EVER ANCIENT, EVER NEW

DOLORES WHELAN

ORIGINAL WRITING

SECOND EDITION
978-1-908024-15-2

A CIP catalogue for this book is available from the National Library.

Published by ORIGINAL WRITING LTD., Dublin, 2010.

Printed by CAHILL PRINTERS LIMITED, Dublin.

*This is dedicated to my father, the late Gerald Whelan,
with gratitude for so much, especially his love of and
devotion to the recovery of the Celtic soul through its
traditional music!*

To Carol, with much love from
your fosterling

ACKNOWLEDGEMENTS

I would like to thank Sean O Boyle and The Columba Press for publishing the first edition of Ever Ancient Ever New in 2006 and so giving voice to this ancient knowledge. I would like to thank my parents the late Gerald and Carmel Whelan for their amazing support of my work and my journey over the years. My thanks to Sue Mosher (Arlington USA) who edited this book as gift to get this work back out in the world. She rearranged the material beautifully so that the book flowed more easily, sensitively suggesting necessary deletions and generally supported this project in a very positive way. My gratitude to Mari Anne Gosling, who proof read the book several times with great clarity and precision; to Susan Quirke for the gifts she brought to my promotional materials; to Fr. Sean O Duinn who has been a constant support of my work and who read the original manuscript.

I would like to thank my many teachers from whom I have learned so much over the past 30 years; all the people people who attended different courses I offered in Celtic Spirituality over the years and whose wise questions allowed me to go deeper into this ancient tradition; those pioneering pilgrims with whom I became familiar with the sacred places in the Irish landscape.

Finally I want to thank my family and many good friends who shared this journey with me and supported me during the times of light and darkness

DOLORES WHELAN
Imbolc 2011

I found *"Ever Ancient Ever New"* a most interesting book, very informative, thought provoking and presents Celtic spirituality with great clarity. It is a wonderful resource book and one we can draw on in our preparation for the celebration of the Celtic Feasts.

Sr Mary Minehan ,
Solas Brid Kildare, Ireland.

Dolores Whelan's book *Ever Ancient Ever New* gives an excellent illustration of her width of knowledge and appreciation of Celtic Spirituality. She makes a careful analysis of the spirit of our age with its materialism and rationalism which she contrasts with an earlier mindset in which mankind is integrated with nature and the feminine mystique receives its due place. This short book draws together the insights of ancient cultures which can lead us into the future

Fr. Sean O Duinn, **Ph.D author of**
Where Three Streams Meet &
The Rites of Brigid Goddess and Saint

Dolores has a knack for mediating both the transformative power hidden in the paradoxical nature of Myth and the mix of joy, earthiness and otherworldliness within the Celtic Soul. Her honest passion for the tradition is evident on every page.

Fionntulach – **Order of Céile Dé Scotland**

These important innovative insights of Dolores Whelan have been hugely transformative in my own life and work. This is truly an inspirational tome.
Between the covers of 'Ever Ancient, Ever New', Dolores directly and succinctly articulates her own bold, daring, call to humanity.
"More than ever, we now need to move towards a deeper understanding of life and from that understanding develop the boldness that dares to follow the heart". *Ever Ancient, Ever New* IS that move and it promises every reader that understanding !

Dr. Noirin Ni Riain
Singer, theologian and musicologist

This second edition of *Ever Ancient Ever New* comes at a time when the outer world appears to be in chaos. Our efforts to fix the world's problems are not deep enough .

People everywhere are looking for solutions and leadership. However, if we really want to transcend these challenges we must stop looking outside for the answers. The answers lie within us,resting inside our ancient memory ready to be awakened if only we allow them. I believe *Ever Ancient Ever New* has the capacity to awaken that ancient memory

RUAIRI MC KIERNAN
Founder of Spunout

In this book Dolores Whelan, speaking with a sure voice from her own Celtic and woman's roots, introduces people in a non superficial way to some of the depth and breadth of ancient Celtic wisdom. Drawing on her own work and appreciation of the Celtic calendar and the Celtic love of the land, of the seasons, of the Divine Feminine and more, she leads not only the reader but the Celtic tradition itself into the rich and profound ways it can contribute to healing humanity in this critical twenty-first century. Very readable, very insightful, very timely.

A "must" book for all who are searching for a deep spirituality today.

MATTHEW FOX,
Theologian and author of many books including *Original Blessing* , *Natural Grace* , *A Spirituality Named Compassion*, *One River, Many Wells*

Dolores Whelan has written a beautiful and accessible guide to the Celtic Spiritual Tradition and she focuses our attention on the wisdom it offers us for today. Rather than nostalgically looking back to times past, she elucidates the key insights and practices that will enhance our spiritual vision for the 21st century. Dolores suggests, "Perhaps it can offer a way forward to people living in the illusion of a separated, disconnected universe, one which has created this myth-less and rudderless society."

MAUREEN O'CONNOR
Transpersonal Psychologist and Psychotherapist,

It is not for antiquarian interest primarily that we look to our Celtic past and what remains of it today like coals under the "smooring" that await a new kindling, but because the shape of our world is wrong and we are being wrongly shaped by it, as so many of our young people realise wildly and desperately.

Noel Dermot O'Donoghue

CONTENTS

INTRODUCTION:
MO SCÉAL FÉIN SCÉAL GACH DUINE[1]

In July 1985, around the time of Live Aid, I returned to Ireland after a three-year sojourn in Canada and California. For several years before my trip, I had been searching for a vision that would bring a unity into my life. I had been on a spiritual path for many years, seeking out different ways and disciplines that would allow me to experience my spiritual self and to experience a connection with God or with the ultimate mystery or reality of the universe. While the spiritual searching resulted in a new understanding of God and the spiritual journey, it seemed separate from the other aspects of my life. It did not impinge on my professional work or on my political or social work. I yearned for a path or vision that would unite the many aspects within myself and my life. My question was, "How could I unite the scientist, the humanitarian, the educator, and the spiritual seeker?"

In 1983, I found a unifying path, at the Institute of Creation Spirituality in Oakland, California, which had been founded by Matthew Fox. This programme offered courses in spirituality that brought together science and spirituality, art and spirituality, social justice and spirituality in an empowering educational process. For two years, I studied spirituality, quantum science, psychology, massage, and healing and awakened to a whole new way of engaging with the universe and all its aspects. I had to unlearn much of what I considered to be "normal" consciousness and normal ways of viewing and relating to the world and life. I was blessed with meeting teachers and thinkers who were at the leading edge of western culture at a perfect time for me.

During my studies in California, my dominant left-brain way of thinking, the result of years of rational scientific work, was greatly challenged. I experienced a wonderful resonance with the writings of the Christian mystics, especially Meister Eckhart and Hildegard of Bingen, and wondered why they never figured in my Catholic education. My limited understanding of God—or how one makes a connection with God—was frequently challenged by my exposure to ceremonies in the Native American and Wicca traditions. In spite of my initial knee jerk-reaction, feelings of guilt at being involved in things "pagan," I experienced a sense of being "at home" in these rituals and ways of praying. I frequently attended a Methodist church in San Francisco, where I was overwhelmed with the sense of joy and vibrancy present in the Sunday service, something I rarely had experienced in 30 years of regular attendance in Catholic churches. I was beginning to see that a whole range of possibilities existed through which the Divine could be mediated and experienced.

Having completed my studies and spent all my money, I decided to return to Ireland. It would have been easy to stay in California, where I had a great network of like-minded people, yet something was drawing me back to Ireland. What drew me back to Ireland was bigger and deeper than my rational mind could understand. It was that aspect, as yet unknown, that supported me in the strange times I encountered on my return. Having left this womb of new ideas where creation-centred spirituality, cosmology, mysticism, psychology, and healing were normal topics of conversation, I arrived back in Ireland, which seemed to me like a different planet. The country was in a deep recession with huge unemployment, and it rained for six weeks. Nobody I spoke to was particularly interested in Christian mystics or cosmology. Everywhere was an air of grim reality that one sensed could easily kill the seeds of spiritual awakening that had been nurtured during that sojourn in California.

So why stay? I was torn between a fear that what had been awakened would be destroyed and a deep urge to share the life-transforming vision that had so utterly awakened my soul. The liberating messages that I had experienced while studying in North America had allowed me to break out of the straightjacket placed on me by the deadness of Irish Catholicism and other forms of colonisation. Having been personally so liberated by my experience of a spirituality that enabled me to experience the interconnectedness of all life, I knew that it was also possible for other people to awaken and be liberated. I wanted to offer this possibility to people in my own country.

This, it seemed, was my next step.

The creation-centred spirituality that I had studied has its roots in the teachings of Meister Eckhart, a 14th century Dominican mystic, and understands the spiritual journey as following four paths: the *Via Positiva*, the way of beauty and blessing; *Via Negativa*, the way of darkness and pain; *Via Creativa*, the way of creativity and new life; and *Via Transformitiva*, the way of being a catalyst for transforming our world. These different streams of the spiritual journey flow into and out of each other constantly. Deeply rooted in a person's daily life, they join spirituality with politics, science, and art, leading to a unified view of life. This integrated cosmology is similar to that held by the primal peoples of many countries. However, in western society, these aspects of life have become separated from each other.

For many years, I taught courses based on these teachings and endeavoured to live them in my own life. It was a wonderfully gratifying experience to watch people open like flowers to their inner beauty, potential, and true spiritual power.

All the while, I mulled over several questions about Ireland, its ancient spiritual past, and the secrets and mysteries it might be holding for us modern people. Did we have an ancient spiritual tradition that was different from the present Christian faith, both Catholic and Protestant? Why did I feel so comfortable and resonate so easily with the teachings and rituals I experienced with the Native American people that I had met?

In 1986, I was given a gift of two tickets to visit Newgrange, an ancient megalithic monument, on December 22, one of the days of the winter solstice. Never having been to Newgrange before, I was very excited and went with a huge sense of anticipation. That morning, I had the privilege of being present when the sun entered the central chamber or womb, and I was allowed to take part in a 5,000-year-old ritual. I was completely overwhelmed and awed by the experience and knew that something significant had happened. Although at that time, I did not have the conscious awareness or the language to fully express what had taken place, some part of me knew that a doorway had been activated or opened. Now I understand that this was an initiation into the land of Ireland and its ancient mysteries.

In September 1988, myself and some friends were asked to accompany a Native American teacher, Dyanni Yahoo, on a journey around some of Ireland's ancient holy places. I agreed, even though I had never been to most of these places. It was a life-changing experience for me to journey with this woman who was so at home within herself, so centred in the moment. She had a quality of serenity and peace that I had seldom encountered before. In her company, I cried buckets of tears, not tears of sadness for something conscious, but tears of deep homesickness or even soul sickness. Being in her presence and feeling her sense of connectedness allowed me to experience my lack of connection with myself and my land and my spiritual tradition. I did not really have a clear sense of what was happening at that time. I only knew that I had a deep sense of peace and of being at home in her presence. Later in September, I made my first pilgrimage to the island of Iona off the west coast of Scotland. Even as I took the ferry from Fionnphort on the island of Mull, I felt what I later came to know as the pull of Iona. I was overwhelmed by the energy on the island, and my Celtic soul was further awakened from its deep slumber.

In July 1989, I attended a week-long course in Celtic spirituality taught by Father Seán Ó Duinn. His focus was the Celtic Christian tradition, which opened for me a whole new perspective on the Christian story. One of the many gifts I received from Seán, who has since been a mentor to me, was the connection of the Christian tradition with its pre-Christian Celtic roots. He also spoke of the importance of the connection of the Celtic tradition with the Megalithic cultures that predated them and of the Celto-megalithic culture that emerged from the synthesis of these two rich traditions. Gradually, the richness and the vastness of the traditions from which I had emerged

4

were unfolding before my eyes. I was rediscovering the depth of the spiritual ground from which I had been cut off. It was no wonder I had felt disconnected.

Since that time, I have been journeying with the Celtic spiritual tradition in many different ways. This journey has involved reading and study, spending time in the natural world, learning to listen to the land, to see, like Patrick Kavanagh, that there is no part of the natural world that isn't also a part of Eden, learning to perceive the mountain behind the mountain, visiting the ancient sacred places, and learning to pray in new, yet ancient ways. This rich and ever evolving tradition has blessed me with insights, as it slowly shares the spiritual wisdom, the mysteries and rituals that created and sustained a vibrant spiritual people and culture in times past.

I am, however, not nostalgic, being much more interested in the future than in the past. It is neither possible nor desirable to re-inhabit previous ages. I believe it is essential, however, that we now recover those nuggets of spiritual wisdom hidden for so long in the mists of time. This book seeks to uncover some of the wisdom of the Celtic tradition and to suggest how it might contribute to a new life-sustaining spiritual vision for 21st century people living in western society. Thus, this book approaches the Celtic tradition in a heart-centred rather than an academic way.

The Celtic spiritual tradition can be understood as something that is both very ancient and new. It is a way of perceiving reality and the world in its many aspects. It is a way of being in the world. At the heart of the Celtic spiritual tradition is the belief in the sacredness of all life and of a physical world imbued with divine presence. It holds a deep understanding of the interconnectedness of all aspects of life, including the links between the physical and spiritual worlds. Relationships are central and important within this tradition. These ancient beliefs resonate strongly with the 20th century writings of Thomas Berry, who proclaims, "Just now one of the significant historical roles of the primal people of the world is not simply to sustain their own traditions, but to call the entire civilized world back to a more authentic mode of being."[2]

This book endeavours to signpost ways to access and reclaim dimensions of reality that have been marginalised as western society marches toward the goal of endless progress. It names many of the gifts that were part of the life of our ancestors, gifts that are recoverable and possibly useful for us today. It challenges us to see ourselves as ancestors of the future generations and asks us to consider what legacies and gifts we wish to leave for those who will come after us. It offers alternatives to the stories that define life within western society. It asks in differing ways, "What is it from our ancient traditions that if reclaimed, would enable us human beings to awaken to the magnitude and wonder of this world? And might this awakening allow us to live in a more conscious and connected way?"

The Celtic tradition and its understanding of the world are neither sentimental nor romantic, but hold wisdom that is urgently needed by our society. This wisdom needs to be recovered now, before its absence from our lives causes even more serious damage to us and to the planet. It is my hope that this book will facilitate access to those forgotten aspects of ourselves and act as a catalyst in the rekindling of the Celtic soul.

Chapter 2:
GIFTS FROM THE CELTIC TRADITION

When considering the nature of Celtic identity, it is usual to ask the question, "Who were the Celtic people?" This, I believe, is only half the question, because an equally important question is "Who are the Celtic people of today?" Or, to consider the issue in a different way, we want not only to know and understand about Celtic consciousness during historic eras, but also to hear its echoes in our own time and perhaps even tune our hearts and our ears to its refrains.

This book approaches what has become known as Celtic consciousness, or Celto-megalithic consciousness, as it unfolded within Ireland over the millennia, in a conceptual rather than chronological way. While it is possible to trace the arrival of the different races of people to the shores of Ireland in a linear fashion, measuring the diverse influences of these races and their contribution to the spiritual, mythological, and cultural landscape of the people living in Ireland is a more challenging and difficult task. As Seán Ó Duinn points out, "We are not dealing with one exclusive religious system"—nor with one race of people—"but rather with a series of different religions and cultures which have influenced each other"[1] in different and surprising ways. Michael Dames, in *Mythic Ireland*, speaks about how these interactions occur in different strata or layers of the culture:

> In Ireland the myths of previous ages are inclined to hang on and on, till eventually (with or without permission) they become embedded in the consciousness of subsequent eras. It is as though each successive wave of Irish culture is half mesmerized by the myths that it has rejected, and in some form acts out the vanquished beliefs, so imparting to the country a compound psychic charge both subtle and strong.[2]

Trying to unravel the mysteries of these past times and peoples, cultures and spiritual traditions can be frustrating. One can easily get lost in the tangles of an exclusively analytical or chronological approach, yet some exposure to the historical background can improve our understanding of what lies between our era and that of the Celtic ancestors—not just centuries of time, but innumerable streams of thought.

For I believe that what removes ideas from our minds is the distance we place between them and ourselves. Far less important is the amount of linear time that has passed since we heard them or since they informed the reality of life. It is the accretion of new ideas that hides older concepts from our minds, not the simple passing of time. And in the case of the Celts, those contributions begin with the very comprehension of reality—even the nature of time—and extend into the stories, rituals, and relationships that draw humans, the natural world, and the divine mystery together into an unbroken wholeness.

Who Are the Celtic People?

It is possible to define the historical period and people that are referred to as "The Celts" and thus express the nature of a society that existed in a certain time and space, distant and different from the present. While the term *Celtic* has a certain magical, mystic vagueness associated with it, it also refers to a society that definitely existed at one time in Europe. This rather heterogeneous group of people became the dominant force in central Europe from approximately 1000 BCE to 200 BCE, emerging in the Rhineland as a distinctive group of clans or tribes. Theirs was a warrior culture, having much in common with the Indo-European warrior society, yet they also were great storytellers and extremely artistic.

The earliest remnants of Celtic culture and art are dated between 800 and 450 BCE and were found in Halstatt, Austria. A later phase of Celtic artwork (350 BCE) is known as the La Tène culture after the Swiss village where it was found. This artwork is famous for its style of ornamentation—wildly imaginative and formalised decoration of floral patterns together with abstract symbols.

From 800 to 300 BCE, Celtic influence spread to Turkey in the east; to Spain, Portugal, and France in the west; and to Britain and Ireland in the north. During the third century BCE, the power of the Celtic peoples declined as they lost whatever political cohesion and common purpose they once held. They were attacked by the Germanic tribes from the north and the Romans from the south, and after 200 BCE, they retreated to the fringes of Europe.

The main body of Celts is believed to have come to Ireland between the third and fifth centuries BCE. When they arrived, it is thought that they encountered an already spiritual people who had their own religious practices and rites. According to the mythologist T.W. Rolleston, the Celts were a spiritually sensitive people and did not overthrow the beliefs and rituals of the indigenous people; rather they honoured them, gradually absorbing them into their own culture. Rolleston suggests that this cross-cultural event was a two-way process allowing a symbiosis of old and new to take place:

> What is quite clear is that when the Celts got to Western Europe, they found there a people with a powerful priesthood, ritual and imposing religious monuments. . . . The inferences, as I read the facts, seem to be that Druidism in its essential features was imposed upon the imaginative and sensitive nature of the Celt . . . by the earlier population of Western Europe, the Megalithic People.[3]

This symbiosis led to a strengthening of religious practice and the Celts' restoration of the sacred places of the Megalithic people, so-called because of the great stone monuments they had constructed. Rolleston further suggests that Druidism was the religion of the aboriginal inhabitants of Europe but that this was recognised where the Celtic people came in contact with the dolmen builders[4], because this meeting of cultures and spiritual practices carried forward the traditions of those earlier people. The Megalithic people and their spiritual traditions thus played a direct role in the subsequent religious development of

Western Europe, contributing to a unique form of Christianity that, through its Druidic roots, was linked to the indigenous philosophy of humanity.[5]

Celto-megalithic culture

Other evidence attests to the intermingling of cultures and religious traditions on the island of Ireland. While Bru Na Bóinne (Newgrange), which dates back to 3300 BCE, is clearly a megalithic monument, it also is the home of the Dagda and Aonghus Óg, gods of the Celtic era. Seán Ó Duinn suggests that this symbiosis led to the formation of a Celto-megalithic culture.[6] T.W. Rolleston asks, "How can we distinguish among them what is of Celtic and what is of pre-Celtic origin?" He assigns to the Megalithic people the special doctrines, the ritual, and the sacerdotal organisation of Druidism and to the Celtic elements, the personified deities with their zest for learning and speculation.[7]

Celtic Christianity

With the arrival of Christianity in Ireland, we see yet another merging of traditions, leading from the pre-Christian Druidic to the Celtic Christian. For Ó Duinn, this implies a "fluidity of thought," together with continuity and intermingling of religious beliefs and practices.[8]

Qualities associated with gods found their way into the stories of dearly beloved saints. An existing affinity for a cycle of festivals and for sacred sites enriched the emerging understanding and celebration of the Light that had come into the world and kindled the Christian message.

Ireland was not invaded by the Romans and maintained its independence against newcomers until the arrival of the Vikings in the 10th century and the Normans in the 12th century. This gave it the ability, according to Rolleston, to carry "the indigenous Celtic civilisation, institutions, art and literature and the oldest surviving form of the Celtic language across a chasm which separates the antique from the modern world and the pagan from the Christian world, and from there into the modern world."[9]

The evolving Celtic inheritance

Such is the rich and diverse heritage that we as Celtic people carry, the ancestral and genetic stock from which we come. This background influences us, consciously or unconsciously, as we engage with our 21st century world, especially in Ireland, where we still experience an amazing mixture of the modern and the archaic in our daily lives.

However, the Celtic inheritance is not just a historical phenomenon anchored in a clearly defined past time and space, but like all vibrant traditions, it is constantly changing. Just as the Megalithic people eventually came to represent a culture rather than a race, so too when we speak about the Celtic world and its influences, we refer to a cultural vision rather than a narrowly defined country-based ethnic group. This tradition, while holding fast to essential concepts that have survived the centuries, is constantly evolving with time. According to the mythologist Rolleston:

> Race character potent and enduring though it be, is not a dead thing, cast in iron mould and thereafter incapable of change and growth. It is part of a living force of the world, it is plastic and vital. It has hidden potencies with a variety of causes such as felicitous crosses with a different, but not too different stock, or in another sphere the adoption of a new religion or social idea may at any time unlock and bring into action.[10]

The gifts of the Celtic consciousness and culture that blossomed in Halstatt, at La Tène, and in Ireland and the fringes of western Britain during the Celtic Christian period were subsequently shared on the world stage. During the Dark Ages, Celtic monks and philosophers spread their teachings and wisdom to the mainland, paving the way for the eventual renaissance of culture in Europe. Perhaps the time is approaching for another out-flowing of Celtic wisdom and consciousness. For this to be effective in our time, it must be offered as a living tradition, for as Rolleston suggests, "This legacy of Celtic influence needs to be cherished, not as a museum curiosity; nothing could be more opposed to the free spirit and wildness of the Celts."[11]

The Celtic soul arising

The Celtic spirit has been rising steadily for more than 100 years, expressing itself most vividly in the music, dance, poetry, and literature of Ireland. Since the beginning of the 20th century, Ireland has produced an amazing array of world-class writers and literature, quite disproportionate to its size or population. This trend in literature has been accompanied by success in many other artistic fields. Since the 1950s, when the traditional music was in serious decline—in fact on the verge of extinction—a wonderful revival and expansion of this music has unfolded. This started as a grassroots movement with small groups of people who met in different parts of the country to share their love for the music. They played and exchanged tunes and began to celebrate their musical heritage. This humble yet essential beginning eventually grew into the now vibrant and creative expression of Irish and Celtic music that has spread all over the world.

What I find so special about Irish music is its raw vitality, its sheer energy, its spontaneity, and its freedom, which can be experienced at any good informal session of Irish music. During these sessions, the musicians play and dance with each other and with the tunes, creating a symphony of sounds and rhythms that bring both the musicians and the listeners to another plane of consciousness. I believe this is one of the ways that we can touch the Celtic otherworld, that other dimension of consciousness, at this time. This may indeed be the gift that this music offers, albeit unconsciously, to a world jaded by materialism and consumerism. Maybe this is the very thing that makes it so attractive to so many people all over the world. Perhaps it was this otherworld energy and presence that leaped from stage to audience during the first performance of *Riverdance*, causing the unsuspecting audience to abandon the norms of decorum and jump to their feet in celebration of the dynamic and magical energy and of the vitality that pulsed through the space.

This present engagement with the Celtic soul through music, myth, literature, and art may hold the seeds for the next full emergence of the Celtic consciousness in the world. The important questions to ponder now are: How can this already vibrant Celtic spirit, which has touched so much of the western world through its music, literature, and poetry, become a powerful agent for the transformation of consciousness within western society? How might the re-emerging Celtic vision of life with its strong spiritual heart shine a light into the world once again?

Celtic consciousness

Since Celtic consciousness is not confined to those people living in countries once regarded as Celtic, you—no matter where you live—may be holding residues of Celtic consciousness deep within your body and soul, which when activated could add themselves to a growing energy of transformation emerging on the planet. Ploughing in this rich field of consciousness in an open and free way, not clinging to past formats, will, I believe, yield a rich harvest and offer cultural and spiritual nourishment with which to heal the wasteland that is 21st century western society.

Having studied and engaged with materials relating to the pre-Celtic megalithic, Celto-megalithic, and Christian Celtic people and their beliefs for over 20 years, I have identified several themes that run through each of these cultures. These ideas have remained central even as the Celtic tradition evolved—core values and beliefs that underpinned the society and from which its mythic, spiritual, and social framework emerged. While crucial to our understanding of the rich wellsprings of knowledge and wisdom that come to us as gifts from our ancestors in these dark times, many of these myths, beliefs, and ritual practices are presently lying dormant and hidden within our consciousness. Nonetheless, they are very real and simply await a new kindling by us in such unique ways as appropriate for this time. It is absolutely possible for us to recover these gifts from our ancestors and bring them into life again today. Each one of us has this potential, for as the elders of the Hopi peoples have said recently, "Now is the time and we are the ones we have been waiting for!"[12]

Gifts from our ancestors

So what are these gifts that the ancestors of the Celtic lands have to offer the world? How can they can be recovered and used by us at this time?

I have gathered them into five themes:

Nature of reality

An understanding that the unbroken wholeness of the universe is the true basis of the nature of reality and of the world

The interconnectedness of the sacred and the secular worlds, of the invisible and visible worlds, in which the material world or the visible world flows from the spiritual or non-visible world

An understanding that a continuum exists from the physical worlds through many non-physical, yet real worlds, to the ultimate mystery

The ability to visit these non-physical, yet real dimensions of the world and to bring back images and wisdom for use in ordinary life

Mythology and ritual

The gift of story, including the importance of the oral tradition and the ability to listen and to remember story

An understanding of the role of myth in underpinning our reality consciously and unconsciously

The development within each individual of both the facility of *muthos* (as discussed in the next chapter) and that of *logos* through education that engages with both the right and left brain and results in deeper levels of intelligence

The importance of ritual and the creation of rituals for daily life and for significant life transitions

An understanding of the need for true spiritual practice and spiritual initiation at transitional points in life

Honouring the ancient spirit of time

Understanding of different experiences of time, both linear and cyclical, and the importance of stepping out of ordinary time and into the non-linear world of the ever-present now

The ability to inhabit the different energies that present themselves during the eight seasons of the Celtic year and to embrace them as a dance of light in darkness, of feminine and masculine energies engaged in a cosmic cycle in which the seasons of the year parallel the seasons of our lives

Understanding of the central role played by death in the life-death-rebirth continuum of existence

Earth as home and mother

An understanding of the earth as a living, sentient, inherently sacred being

The ability to be present in the natural world, to experience the awe and mystery of the universe, and to access in a tangible way the divine presence in nature

An understanding of *anima loci*, or places of soul in the earth, that hold special energies and where the veil between the worlds is thin

Relationships

The importance of living in right relationship with the earth

Sovereignty and the rightful rule of the king, personifying the central role of right relationships among humanity, the natural world, and the divine order.

An understanding of justice as right relationships rather than legalism

The importance of community: "*Is ar scath a cheile a mhaireann na daoine.*" ("We live in the crook of each other's arm.")

Perhaps we are entering a time when the perennial philosophy that inspired the great Celtic and pre-Celtic teachers, peoples, and cultures will find a new expression in our world. It may be that the recovery of this ancient knowledge, wisdom, and spiritual tradition will enable us to understand both the true nature of reality and our place as humans in the world. It may help us to grasp our deep and intimate connection with the natural world, teaching us how to live in greater harmony, returning vitality to the earth, re-enchantment to the world, and joy into the human heart. What is it that we, modern humans, need to learn, what do we need to awaken, so that the wisdom present within our souls and psyche, within our DNA, can be released and used at this juncture in the evolution of consciousness here on planet earth?

What are the wellsprings deep within our souls from which we can draw inspiration, insights, and courage? How can we access this knowledge, which not only will support us in coping with the challenges of life in 21st century, but also will liberate each of us into the truth of our being as we awaken to the true nature of reality? What can be recovered that will lead us humans to a sense of wholeness and belonging?

At this time, much old and new knowledge is available that can radically change the way we perceive ourselves, the universe, and God. It can help us cope with the challenges of 21st century life and feed the gaping wound in our souls. The following chapters will explore some of these themes and offer ways for us, modern pilgrims, to incorporate these ideas into our daily lives.

Chapter 3:
A DIFFERENT WAY OF KNOWING

We live at a time when ancient esoteric knowledge is being rediscovered. The veiled world of the enduring Celtic imagination is revealing itself as a container for something that is both universally human and divine. We, as people of the Celtic tradition, can reclaim this ancient wisdom, in ways that reflect our individual historical and mythological background.

The merging of the physical, the spiritual, and the imaginal worlds holds a key to understanding the essence of the Celtic mysteries and the Celtic soul. But how are we to access the wisdom of this tradition without embracing one of the primary pillars of that culture—the realm of imagination with its mythic consciousness? Since the Enlightenment, almost four centuries ago, western society has encouraged people to abandon all forms of knowing that do not reflect logical thinking or represent material reality. The confinement of consciousness to the physical and logical has diminished the number of possible worlds in which to experience life. We have chosen to deny the non-physical worlds, to ignore the wisdom of our ancestors, and to silence the voices of the non-human worlds. Yet within the human heart, the memory of all these worlds is present and is available to us. But how can we reach into the human heart in a world that values head knowledge over heart wisdom and truth?

Mythic knowing

In contemporary western culture, where the rational, logical, and analytical way of knowing, *logos*, is supremely valued, even the word myth conjures up something that is considered at best to be an entertaining story from the past and at worst to be untrue and unworthy of serious consideration. Within the rational scientific ideology, the belief that non-physical, yet real worlds may exist is treated with contempt. Yet this overvaluing of the rational, analytical way of knowing is itself both a central weakness and a major cause of many problems encountered in western society today; as psychologist Alfred Adler once noted, "what makes madness is literalism."[1] This *logos*-driven world excludes *muthos* (the Greek word from which we derive the word *myth*) as a valid way of knowing.

So what exactly is meant by *muthos*? The root of this word is *mu*, whose meanings include silence, secrets, hidden, and arcane. *Muthos* is also related to speech and to the oral tradition. According to Seán Ó Duinn, behind this way of knowing, *muthos* is the mystery in the story and the secret hidden in the story, which even if not fully understood from a cognitive perspective brings the listener into relationship with the cosmos.[2] Oral storytelling thrives on poetic images and sounds that evoke the listener's imagination and open up new worlds.

Muthos as a way of knowing is associated with the right hemisphere of the brain, while *logos* is associated with the left hemisphere. The right brain is the realm of intuition, where images rather than words dominate, where metaphors are readily understood and fantasy is possible. It supports our dreaming and facilitates our opening to the spiritual and mystical realms within ourselves and within the world. The left brain is the realm of logical, analytical knowing, where facts dominate and words have literal meanings. In this realm, information is processed in a linear, sequential way. Here we remember facts, know how to spell, understand abstract language and reasoning, and delight in mathematical analysis. In a healthy, integrated society, both these different aspects of the brain are developed and the knowledge present in both is valued. The challenge today is how to bring balance to this present asymmetry: What is needed in order that *muthos*, this right-brain way of knowing and gateway to the realms of the imagination and soul, might be understood and valued?

The creative spirit within

Once we acknowledge the importance of developing the creative and spiritual aspects within every person—not just those recognised as professional artists—a new challenge arises: Creativity cannot be taught. However, it is possible to nurture the artistic spirit and allow it to flourish by creating an environment where it is safe for the latent creativity and imagination within each person to emerge.

The creative spirit needs silence and space where it can withdraw from the endless noise of everyday living and the dominant voices in the culture, where it can hear the truth of its own inner knowing. The spiritual seeker also requires this silence and space. The seeker must pull life's questions down from the surface into a deeper place where true wisdom might be found. Here the capacity to wonder and ponder is crucial and is greatly enhanced by the use of the imagination. How difficult this can be in the present society, which seems preoccupied with productivity and with such a relentless way of life.

This is not to say that we should no longer value the brightness and the speed of intellectual knowledge and its contributions to our health and material well-being. However, to nourish the creative spirit and the spiritual essence within the human heart, it is necessary to validate the gifts present in the right brain and to honour its particular way of perceiving reality. The fullness of wisdom requires the inclusion of the slower, quieter knowing of the heart. To access this realm, we must be open to the knowledge that can emerge only in the softness of twilight, in the stillness of the natural world, and in the stories told around a fire. Here lie the abilities that will lead us into deeper levels of knowing and deeper realms of life.

This is where our journey into the wisdom of the Celtic tradition must begin.

The three worlds

The presence of the three worlds is a central and defining aspect of the Celtic cosmology—the physical or material world, the imaginal world, and the spiritual world. For the Celtic people and other primal peoples, the physical world emerges from the spiritual, and the visible world emerges from the invisible. The imaginal world is the region between the physical or material world and the spiritual world or the ultimate mystery or source. This is the Celtic otherworld, Tír na nÓg, also known as the *mundus imaginalis* of the Celts. This otherworld is not an archetype produced by the unconscious mind, nor is it a product of fictional imagination. It is a dimension of reality that exists within the world and within the psyche or soul, the inner dimension of self. The Irish expression *"Ta Tír na nÓg ar cúl an tí"*—the otherworld is right behind your house—alerts us to the fact that, while this otherworld resides in another dimension, it is paradoxically right beside us. As many of the myths tell us, this otherworld is an extension of the physical world and is all around us. So how does one get to this otherworld?

To access this world, a person must vacate the habitual, rational mind and move into the realm of psyche and intuitive knowing. One must step outside the linear space-time continuum and left-brain consciousness. To inhabit this place requires attunement to the inner world, which is not something available at will, but a skill developed through constant practice. It requires a journey from the head to the heart, for as poet Patrick Kavanagh reminds us, "God cannot catch us unless we stay in the unconscious room of our hearts."[3] Assisting with that journey is a cache of stories and rituals that surface from the mythic realm. When we employ them, we may grasp, with mythologist Joseph Campbell, that "the first function of mythology—myths and mystical rituals, sacred songs and ceremonial dances—is to awaken in the individual a sense of awe, wonder and participation in the inscrutable."[4]

As we make this journey, we can glimpse the eternal otherworld and develop the capacity to see into the essential nature of things. We move into a different realm within the psyche where it is possible to inhabit the past, present, and future in this current moment. This is the world where myths are created and archetypal energies reside. Here the mythical world, the world of spirit and soul, awakens and offers us its wisdom and gifts. Spending time in this world nourishes our mythic consciousness, which in turn feeds the hunger in our souls. In this place, life is free from the limitations of the physical world of time and space. Here the imagination, as a way of perceiving the world, opens up and creates stories and scenarios where the possible and the impossible meet and mingle. Fionntulach, a monk in the Céile Dé spiritual tradition, believes that spending time in this realm and developing the consciousness found there leads to greater soul knowledge (*coinneach*), which in turn leads us to the realm of spirit and ultimately to spiritual awakening.[5]

Because the ability to access these inner, spiritual realms is so underdeveloped in our society, many people dismiss both their existence and the energies and beings present there as figments of the imagination. Exploring the mythological world of the Celtic people can act as an antidote to this sceptical and reductionist worldview.

Redeeming mythology

In order to redeem myth and restore its role in sustaining a healthy society, we need to distance ourselves from the disparaging definitions of myth found in most modern dictionaries. We need to reclaim the more ancient and accurate understanding of myth and validate the existence of the mythological world. People often think of myths as stories from a previous time that may or may not have relevance for us today. Because myths embody eternal truths rather than empirical truths, their stories may or may not be true at all levels. Yet the myths that survive into the present time, those myths embodied in our DNA, are those stories that gave meaning to the lives of our ancestors and that still have validity. It is important and often difficult for us modern humans, chained as we are to literalism, to realise that whether or not a character actually existed in historical time is not central to the relevance of a particular myth. A story that is carried forward through history and becomes part of the mythology of the people is one that contains insights and wisdom important to the development of the culture and the psyche of the society. These myths still occupy space within our psyche.

Many philosophers who value a mythological perspective describe myth as representing primordial truths expressed at the highest level comprehensible to human beings. For the Hopi people of North America, their language divides material not into past, present, and future tenses, but into the manifest world and the world of potential. This is similar to what American spiritual philosopher David Spangler describes when he speaks of the implicit and explicit orders of reality.[6] For the Hopi people, both the future and the mythic past exist in the present moment, within the implicate order. That is, they exist in this moment but in a dimension of time and space that is different from the linear time of the physical world.

John Matthews, in *The Celtic Shaman*, also speaks about myths and mythic consciousness as occupying different aspects of one's psyche rather than being vestiges of former times. He writes, "When we move into those regions of our psyche through meditation or trance and meet characters from the historical past, we are actually meeting with archetypal energies present within our psyches, in a dimension outside of linear time and space."[7] Such travels can offer insights and wisdom that expand the world of possibilities beyond the physical realm and offer a way forward to people living in the illusion of a separated, disconnected universe, one that has created what seems like a mythless and rudderless society.

The western scientific myth

Though today's western culture may appear mythless, I believe that society is always consciously or unconsciously influenced by some mythology. The myth that presently dominates life in western society is one of endless growth and consumerism. This myth associates wealth with money and equates success exclusively with material possessions. It places the human being and individualism at the centre of the universe. The earth is seen as an endless resource of raw materials and a dumping ground for waste products. The rights of all other species are seen as subordinate to those of humans, while the reality of the earth as a living, sentient organism with its own unfolding rhythm is completely denied. The world perceived in this way has no connection with any other dimensions of reality, because the physical world is understood to be the only world that exists, complete unto itself.

This very limited experience of life has emerged from the overdevelopment of the rational mind and the accompanying underdevelopment of the intuitive, imaginal way of knowing. The scientific model of learning and knowledge reigns supreme in nearly all disciplines. Even religion subscribes to this model. The truth on offer from both scientific and spiritual authorities is unquestioned and often seen as absolute. When we examine it closely, though, we see that what underpins this model is a set of assumptions from which a story emerges about the world and how it functions. It is, in other words, a mythology—but one that has been created by the rational, analytical mind, disconnected from much of the knowledge, wisdom, and insights from past times.

Since the time of the Enlightenment in the 17th century, the western scientific tradition has endeavoured to break away from its pre-scientific past and to forge ahead with the creation of a brave new world. In this world, humans would be free from the forces of nature and from what science considered to be superstitions. At the core of this worldview, from the time of Isaac Newton until the early 20th century, was the concept of a universe composed of separate units of matter, atoms, which interacted through collisions with each other. The fundamental reality of the world thus was understood as essentially dependent on the relationships among discrete and separate entities.

With the advent of quantum physics, the work of Albert Einstein and others, a new story of the universe has emerged. It has been shown that within the universe, at the sub-atomic level, everything exists as energy in motion and in relationship with everything else. This new story has revealed an absolutely interconnected universe.

Yet in spite of these revelations, most present-day institutions are organised and operate from a Newtonian perspective of reality, one of partition and isolation. One consequence has been a tendency to compartmentalize life into its various aspects and attempt to keep them separate. Education was split into spiritual and scientific programmes, in contrast with earlier curricula that included scientific, artistic, philosophical, and spiritual components. In time, society came to believe that it was possible to separate life into the secular and the spiritual, into the scientific and the artistic.

The core values of this society became identified with the physical, material world and dismissed as irrelevant or merely curious the spiritual, non-material world. As a consequence, the philosophical and spiritual underpinnings of life and society were marginalised, while the predominant forces created ideologies and organised life based on a shallow and inaccurate view of the true nature of the universe. The world derived from this mythology believes that "this is it" and desperately wants to hold on to the physical manifestations of life and wealth. This thinking leads to over-identification with *eros*, love of life, while being terrified of *thanatos*, the experience of death. This approach loves light and fears darkness, identifies with summer while wishing to banish winter. Living in this way creates a world of duality, where some aspects are idealised, while their opposites are demonised. Such a world defies reality and is simply not sustainable.

Of those who live so disconnected from the past and unconcerned about the future, psychologist C.G. Jung wrote, "The person who thinks that he can live without myth or outside of it, like one uprooted, has no true link either with the past or with the ancestral life that continues within the contemporary human society. This plaything of his reason never grips his vitals."[8] A society made up of such individuals is one out of touch with its mythic foundation, "the mythless shell, a house without gods,"[9] like that found, according to Michael Dames, in Samuel Beckett's play *Endgame*.

What ails us?

The scientific, rational worldview may excel at inventing labour-saving machines, setting exchange rates, and curing diseases of the body, but it has shown little ability to ease the pains and longings of the soul and society. Reacting to and recognising the limitations of the mechanistic, atomistic worldview, many poets, writers, and painters have championed the importance of the natural world as the ground of being for humans and have maintained contact with the inner world.

Yet this does not seem to be enough. The sense of brokenness that permeates much of the world carries a Humpty-Dumpty-like fear that neither we nor "all the king's horses and all the king's men" can put it together again. We ask in so many ways "What ails us?" and hear the answer, "The world is crying to be made whole again." I believe wholeness will return only when that which has been torn apart is back brought together. It will come when that which has been marginalised is reintegrated into the whole.

Restoring wholeness to ourselves and our world requires that each of us—not just the professional artists and spiritual teachers—experience, honour, and integrate all the parts of ourselves, allowing them to create balance and harmony within our lives. We need to relearn how to inhabit the inner world and the outer world, the timeless and the temporal world, the ancient and the new worlds. Entering the spiritual dimensions of the world through appropriate rituals and ceremonies will help recreate this wholeness. Into this fragmented world, the gift of the Celtic imagination is offered as a healing balm filled with true reality and possibility, for as John Keats reminds us, "I am certain of nothing but of the holiness of the Heart's affections, and the truth of Imagination."[10] Exploring the world of Celtic mythology will, I believe, offer great wisdom to all who seek a way out of the present spiritual and ecological wasteland. It will be particularly potent for those who have an ethnic, spiritual, or cultural connection to this tradition.

The gifts of Celtic mythology

Because the world of myth exists outside the laws of the physical material world, it can transcend the norms of what is considered possible. Inhabiting the world of myth helps to suspend the normal rational judgements and leads to an expansion in our perception of what is possible. When we return from this world of myth, the material world does not appear as fixed or solid as before. We learn that "myth and ritual loosen the grip of the temporal world upon the human spirit."[11] The mythological stories are large enough to hold the ambiguities present in the many polarities encountered in life—life and death, youth and old age, light and darkness, success and failure, masculine and feminine energies. Engaging with and entering into the heart of the myths allows us to encounter in a safe way these difficult elements of our earthly reality and obtain insight and support. Ironically, for contemporary western society with its fear of all forms of death, the Celtic myths of life, death, and rebirth may offer the human psyche healing of its fear of death.

The story of the *Battle of Mag Tuiread* is a classic tale of the battle between good and evil, between light and dark forces. The battle is set at the time of Samhain, an auspicious time in the Celtic calendar. It is the gap between the end of one year and the beginning of another year, a time of change and chaos. In this myth, Balor, the Formorian, representing the forces of darkness, kills Nuada, the king of the Tuatha Dé Danann, who represents the forces of light. Later Lugh, the new king of the Tuatha Dé Danann, kills Balor. The relationship between Lugh and his grandfather Balor indicates that these forces of light and darkness are interconnected and are both present within human consciousness. The story suggests a gradual transformation of ignorance and darkness by light and intelligence, where both the light and darkness are needed for this transformation to happen.

Success and failure, death and life are understood very differently at a soul level than at the level of ego. The many tragic stories like *The Children of Lir, The Sons of Tuirreann,* and *The Exile of the Sons of Uishneach* demonstrate that misfortune has always been part of the human condition. They can help us understand that, in spite of what we may believe, not everything is within the control of the rational mind and the longing of the ego. We may awaken to a story that is larger than the story for which the human ego longs and begin to see the soul journey that is being lived within one's human passage.

Celtic mythology abounds with stories where humans make journeys to the otherworld and stories of visitations from the otherworld into this physical world. Some of these journeys are pleasant; others are not. Time spent in the otherworld is not like time spent in the material world. The stories of Tír na nÓg and Tír na mBan are particularly important because of what they suggest about the need to integrate the gifts of the otherworld with the realities of human material existence.

The story of Oisin and his enticement to Tír na nÓg by Niamh, daughter of the king of the land of eternal youth, is well known to many people. Oisin willingly goes with Niamh and enjoys all the pleasures and delights of this place for what seems to him a short time. He decides to return to the normal world, only to discover that his eternal youth exists only in that other world. When he comes in contact with the physical world, he is again under the influence of linear time. He now discovers that time has moved on in the physical world, that he has been away for 300 years, and that no one remembers him.

In another journey tale, Bran, King of Ireland, travels with his many followers past the ninth wave and arrives at Tír na mBan, the island of women. Here their every need is met, and life is full of pleasure with no earthly worries. After a time, they weary of the pleasures and decide to go home. When they return to Ireland, they realise that several hundred years of linear time have elapsed.

Both of these stories depict the realm of the unconscious as a place where the feminine energy of being is dominant. These places, while beautiful and seductively comforting, are places that humans should visit only for short periods to gain insights and knowledge, which must then be brought back to this world and used to support the human journey. In these stories, the people are unaware of the vast quantity of linear time that has passed in the physical world while they have been in the otherworld. Staying in the otherworld too long can result in contact with this world being lost and opportunities to integrate the received messages being missed.

In Irish mythology, the primacy of the feminine dimension is reflected in the many myths about the sovereignty of the land, where the feminine is understood as a personification of the fertility of the land and is expressed in the form of a goddess. When a king is inaugurated, he must ritually marry the local goddess representing the sovereignty of the land. If his rule is just, the land will bring forth its bounty, and the king will be deemed successful. But his success depends on his ability to be in right relationship with the feminine, the goddess of the land. What an important message this holds for our time!

Meditation: A journey to the Celtic otherworld

The capacity to journey to the otherworld, the visionary place within, the imaginal dimension, is still present in human beings. All we need is the willingness to move out of our heads and into our hearts. This meditation will guide you into the Celtic otherworld, where you will find inspiration and guidance to support you in your daily life. You may want to record this meditation or have someone read it to you, with pauses to allow time for you to respond.

Become aware of your body sitting on a chair, cushion, or couch or lying on the floor. Move your body so that you are completely comfortable. Bring your attention to your breath, not the thought of your breath, but the actual reality of your breath, as it comes into your body and as it leaves your body. Be aware of the sensations as your breath enters and leaves your nostrils. Focus your attention on your exhalation, breathing out as deeply as you can. Be aware of the space created by the out-breath, pause in that awareness, and allow that space to be filled with the next incoming breath.

Repeat this process five times and with each exhalation allow yourself to sink deeper and deeper into the centre of your own being. As you settle into this deep place within yourself, you may sense a question emerging, a question about some aspect of your present life, a question whose answer is not readily available to you through ordinary waking consciousness. This question requires that you make a journey into the other realms within yourself.

See, feel, or know that you are walking along a beach. You hear the sounds of the waves ebbing and flowing. You hear the birds' cries. You smell the sea salt. You feel the breeze on your skin. You see the sun shining on the water as you walk along the beach. In this place, all your senses are heightened, and you feel fully awake. Everything looks so beautiful!

After walking for some time, you see a small boat at the edge of the water. It can be any kind of boat that you desire. What type of boat is it? Somehow you feel guided to get into this boat and push out from the shore. You have no fear, because some part of you knows that you are completely safe on this journey. You feel at ease and relaxed as you guide the boat out and away from the shore. You feel a sense of exhilaration and adventure as you move in harmony with the waves, leaving the shoreline further and further behind you.

You become aware of having travelled some distance now, and you wonder to yourself if you have yet journeyed out over the ninth wave, a place you know to be a gateway into the other dimensions of reality. As you look out from the boat, you notice a small island ahead of you. This island seems to call you towards it. You set your course and head towards this island wondering what gifts and treasures it might hold for you, what insights or answers it might offer for your question.

After some time, you arrive at the shore, where you land the boat easily. You spend a few moments feeling the sand under your feet and sensing your connection with this place. You breathe deeply, allowing the breath to strengthen your connection with this magical island. You wonder, "To where in this beautiful island am I being drawn?" You wait until you sense the direction that you need to follow. Guided by your intuition, you begin to move with ease and safety along your chosen path. Be aware of everything you hear and see and sense and smell as you travel in this beautiful place. What birds, what animals do you notice? What trees or plants call to you? What do you notice out of the corner of your eye? Be aware of everything as you walk through the island, holding your question clearly in your awareness.

Soon, you come to a place that seems to say to you, "This is my place!" What type of place is it? Is it a forest? Or is it beside a lake or stream? Or is it a stony place that calls you? Once you have found your place, you sit quietly, allowing yourself to be fully present to all that is seen and unseen here. And as you do, you feel yourself opening up to the deep presence that pervades this place.

While you are sitting here, centred within that deep place in yourself and conscious of your breath, you open yourself to receive insights and intuitions about your question and your journey in life at this time. Pay attention to every thought, image, symbol, insight, memory, or body sensation that arises. Allow yourself to be surprised. Don't judge anything! Be open to what is offered to you. I invite you to stay a while here to receive and to gather all the insights and answers you need for your journey at this time.

Now it is time to leave. You bid farewell to this special place. You give thanks for all that you have received.

You make your way back to the beach and to your boat. Getting into your boat, you begin your journey back to the mainland. You travel back over the waves with ease and a sense of exhilaration, and very soon you arrive back at the shore. You get out of the boat and walk along the beach feeling a sense of deep gratitude for the gifts and insights you have received. Now you become aware of your body sitting on the chair, the cushion, or the couch or lying on the floor. You become aware again of your breath—the inhalation and the exhalation—and you become aware of the space around you. Now bring your attention fully back to this present reality and this present moment. You may wish to write down the insights and answers you received.

Know that you can travel to this place within yourself anytime you choose and receive the insights and the answers you need.

Mythology—food for the soul

Unlike religious dogma, myth is not a fixed entity. Myth allows for flexibility of interpretation, changing and growing with one's ability to inhabit and understand it. I found, as I gradually developed the right-brain consciousness within myself, that my ability to understand and inhabit the myths expanded, revealing more of their secrets. Mythologists Alwyn and Brinley Rees aptly say, "It is a function of mythology to confound the guardian spirit of reason so that finite man may glimpse the infinite which lies beyond the confines of the cosmos."[12] Myth facilitates the creation of a deeper story within us and a larger context within which to locate our lives. This can shape and sustain our emotional attitudes and our responses to daily living.

Nature and mythology are the sustaining foods of the soul, as Patrick Kavanagh reminds us in his poem "Canal Bank Walk": "For this soul needs to be honoured with a new dress woven from green and blue things and arguments that cannot be proven."[13] The development of the capacity to inhabit that world of mythical knowing allows us humans to open up and engage more fully with the world in which we move and breathe.

The kernels of ancient wisdom present within Celtic mythology are emerging at this time from the forgetfulness of many, many centuries. It is possible that this wisdom will interact with the new insights present in the new unitive, interdependent cosmological story and result in a fresh blossoming of the essential wisdom of this ancient tradition.

Chapter 4:

RECOVERING THE
GOD-INTOXICATED CELT

Teilhard de Chardin once remarked, "We are not human beings having a spiritual experience; we are spiritual beings having a human experience."[1] This idea would certainly resonate with the peoples who lived in the Celtic lands over the centuries. These people understood that their fundamental nature was spiritual and that the physical world they inhabited was an epiphany of that spiritual essence. Life simply could not be separated into spiritual and secular. There was only life—in its many manifestations, interconnected and flowing into, out from, and through myriad dimensions. The Celts' belief in the intertwining of the different dimensions of reality was reflected in a widely used expression, "Tír na nÓg [the otherworld] is in your own back yard, and heaven is a foot above your head." The spiritual life was grounded in the daily life of the individual and the tribe or community and also in the yearly round of the seasons with their celebrations and rituals. Enriching it were places of special inspiration in the landscape and able companions for the journey.

Prayer—the daily companion

The presence of the spiritual dimension in daily life is clearly recorded and expressed in the multitude of prayers, invocations, and blessings that have come down to us through the work of Alexander Carmichael in Scotland and Douglas Hyde and Diarmuid Ó Laoghaire in Ireland. These prayers and invocations reveal a culture that was deeply aware of the central role played by the spiritual dimension of life. A selection helps demonstrate how each different situation might have its own prayer:

A *night prayer*
May our bed of sleep be a bed safe for repose and
may we arise in the morning in the permanent protection of God.[2]

Morning prayer
I rise up with God, may God rise up with me.
The arm of God around me, when going about
and in bed and at rising.[3]

Moon prayer
Glory be to you, O God of the Elements,
for the shining lantern of the ocean;
may your own hands be guiding my rudder
and your mysterious love behind the waves.[4]

The following prayer reflects the invocation of heavenly and
cosmic forces for protection:

May Mary bless you and may God bless you. . . .
May the bright moon and the sun bless you.
May the eastern man and western man bless you.
And last of all may I myself bless you.[5]

For these people, prayer was a natural aspect of one's life.
It was normal to invoke support and protection from a higher
power or other realms for the tasks undertaken in the course of
a day. This constant use of prayers and rituals was used to build
up an awareness of God or the divine presence, so that daily
life could become a vehicle through which one could awaken
to unity with God. Theologian John Macquarrie speaks about
the intense sense of divine presence that was a core belief within
the Celtic spiritual tradition: "The Celt was very much a God-
intoxicated man whose life was embraced on all sides by the
divine Being. But this presence was always mediated through
some this-world reality."[6] This was an egalitarian spirituality in
which everyone had the right and responsibility to develop their
spirituality. What made this possible was the Celts' capacity to

see past the material world and experience its spiritual essence, a capacity developed through years of spiritual practices and facilitated by their immediate connection with the world of nature. Along with a belief in the essentially spiritual nature of all creation, they believed that reality constituted a continuum that extended from the physical, material realm through non-material realms to the space where pure spirit resides. As described in the previous chapter, it was considered both possible and desirable that people visit these non-material realms to find insights and inspiration.

Recovering the spiritual dimension of life

It is sometimes difficult for those of us living within the mindset of contemporary western culture to grasp the depth of spiritual insight present within the consciousness of former times. We imagine that the evolution of consciousness has occurred in a straight line and that humankind's current position represents the ultimate achievement for human consciousness. In fact, the human consciousness present in western society today is so completely skewed in favour of rational knowing as to be seriously out of balance and lacking real wisdom.

So is it possible or desirable that we, people living in the 21st century, should reconnect with the spiritual dimension of life and recover the spiritual tools necessary to engage with it? I believe that it is not only desirable, but one of the most urgent tasks of this time. Developing the non-rational, intuitive aspects of self not only facilitates connections with the imaginal world, but also allows us to be present in and engage with, the natural world in a more fundamental way. Many of the Celtic Christian monks, building on the pre-Christian traditions, understood the natural world to be equally important in the pursuit of holiness as the scriptures. I believe there is an urgent need within our society for people to take time to go apart from the noise of daily living and connect with self and spirit in the quietness of the natural world, to quiet down sufficiently to know who they are, where they are, and what their real needs are. The following poem, "Lost" by David Wagoner, is based on a Native

American teaching story used for instruction of young adults and speaks powerfully to all of us seeking direction about the need to stand still in order to know:

> Stand still. The trees ahead and bushes beside you
> Are not lost. Wherever you are is called Here,
> And you must treat it as you would a powerful stranger,
> Must ask permission to know it and be known.
> The forest breathes. Listen. It answers,
> I have made this place around you.
> If you leave it, you may come back again, saying Here.
> No two trees are the same to Raven.
> No two bushes are the same to Wren.
> If what a tree or a branch does is lost on you,
> You are surely lost. Stand still. The forest knows
> where you are. You must let it find you.[7]

However, given the damage that has happened to both the natural world and to the ability of the human to perceive the natural world in its complexity, I wonder if it is possible for us humans ever again to see the world in its pristine wholeness. Perhaps the only way for each of us to begin is to open up to the natural world with child-like wonder.

Opening to the real world

If we are ever to recover the throbbing awareness of divine presence in the natural world, the first step must be to slow down. Slow down enough to become fully aware of the world around us, to see, hear, smell, taste, and touch the reality of the world in which we live. This deceleration may bring us sufficiently into the present moment that the numinous dimension of the natural world may become manifest.

Engaging in this way can lead us into a different relationship with the natural world. When we spend quiet time in nature, we step outside social norms and concerns, allowing them to drop away so that we can be in communion with the universe, with the landscape, the mountains, the trees, the grasses, the sea, the birds, and the animals. In nature, it is possible to move outside the small self, with its many mundane concerns, and access greater and deeper aspects of self. Such a shift opens us to the possibility that the vast universe may break into our consciousness and transform it. Allowing the primal aspects of self to emerge, where they can be experienced and integrated, can heal so much of what ails us, cosseted as we are and devoid of authentic contact with the natural world.

Intentional walks in nature

When we reawaken to nature's beauty, power, and wisdom, we remember why the wild places must be preserved and why the earth must be honoured. How then do we begin to be present in the natural world? Where can we go to access it, especially if we live in the city? While the countryside can be wilder and more primal than city parks, it is nevertheless possible to engage with the natural world anywhere. All that is needed is your commitment to wake up and a willingness to stay awake. It can be helpful to choose to be on your own, to walk slowly with awareness, and to use all your senses to engage with your surroundings. Become aware of the earth beneath your feet, and notice the presence of the life-force. Allow yourself to experience each living thing with the wonder of a child seeing it for the first time. Allow yourself to be surprised!

You can also try "listening" to what the natural world has to teach you. In this practice, you walk with awareness for a certain time, while holding an issue or question in your mind. As you walk, notice where your attention is drawn. Pay attention to the messages being offered to you by everything you see and hear. Allow the world to be your teacher! Later you can record your reflections and insights.

Beginning in these simple ways has the potential to open you up to a new relationship with the world and change your perception forever, for as William Blake said, "If the doors of perception were cleansed every thing would appear to man as it is, infinite. For man has closed himself up, till he sees all things thro' narrow chinks in his cavern."[8] This larger perception has

41

the capacity to awaken in us what is needed at this time, so that the world can again become an enchanted planet.

The sacred earth

The Celtic and pre-Celtic people, like all primal people, understood the sacred nature of the land out of which they emerged and that sustained them. They understood the land as a living body infused with spirit and soul where nothing was impersonal. This awareness of the energies present in different places was foundational in choosing land for different activities and uses. They knew that the landscape had certain places where the presence of spirit was tangible in a special way. Here, the place-soul, or *anima loci*, could be experienced by anyone who had developed the necessary sensitivity. At these places, the human-divine connection was more tangible, and the veil between the worlds was thinner. Because of their special energy, such sites were chosen for temples, churches, and other places of worship. When people came, tuned into, and acknowledged the *anima loci*, the energies present in the place were called forth more fully. The unseen spiritual energies became more accessible to human awareness. As people responded to the energies present there, those energies became more embodied in the place, always in a way specific to that location. Many western people have lost the deep connection with land necessary to hold this awareness, yet I believe there is still a strong connection within the Irish psyche with the idea of place as sacred.

Ireland's sacred landscape

Ireland has probably the greatest number of functioning sacred sites and places in Western Europe. Many are visited regularly by people performing the ancient art of pilgrimage, also known in Ireland as *turas*. On the last Sunday in July each year, thousands of people re-enact the ancient practice of climbing Croagh Patrick in County Mayo. Each year, thousands go on pilgrimage to Lough Derg, while many people all over the country make pilgrimages at certain times to particular holy wells in their own localities. Until recent times, people often walked to the top of a local hill at sunrise on Easter Sunday to see the sun dance as it rose on that special morning. A special pilgrimage in which people walk the 15 stations of St. Colmcille's *turas* is still celebrated each year in Glencolmcille in County Donegal on June 9th, his feast day.

As with spending time in the natural world, visiting sacred places creates an increased awareness of the various energies present in different locations. As we humans become more attuned to the earth and her subtleties, we may challenge the modernist view that "recognizes no real spiritual or even physical differences of note between places" and in doing so creates "a random series of virtually uninhabitable 'nowheres.'"[9] The continued vitality of such ancient pilgrimage practices—co-existing with the modernity of 21st century Ireland—reflects the persistence of older mythic layers within contemporary Irish life and the possibility of recovering more of that connection with the sacred landscape.

The *anam cara* tradition

An additional practice in the Celtic spiritual tradition is that of *anam cara*, which offers great support on the spiritual journey. *Anam cara* in the Irish language means soul friend. The Celtic people, both Christian and pre-Christian, understood that the authentic spiritual journey was arduous and needed support. An *anam cara* is a person, who like you, is on a spiritual journey, but may be further along that journey and, therefore, in a position to guide you along your path. The *anam cara* accompanies another person in their inner journey but not in the role of priest, pastor, or therapist. So important was the *anam cara* relationship that Brigid of Kildare once said that "anybody without a soul friend is like a body without a head."[10] This person will have developed a certain level of spiritual and psychological understanding and can be a trusted companion who holds a safe space for you so that you can share the intimate details of your own spiritual journey. The relationship may be formal or informal, maintained on an ongoing basis or held within a certain timeframe.

Rekindling the ashes

There is a huge spiritual hunger in the lives of many people and a genuine search for a deeper and more authentic spiritual life. Responding to this spiritual hunger requires commitment, dedication, discernment, and spiritual companions. While many people look towards the East for meaningful spiritual pathways, more people are becoming aware of the riches of the Celtic tradition that "are like coals under 'smoorings' awaiting a new kindling."[11] Many of the spiritual practices from the Celtic tradition, such as simple prayers, invoking the help of the unseen world in one's daily life, invoking protection, making pilgrimages to sacred places, and spending quiet time in the natural world can be incorporated effectively into the spiritual journey of the present-day seeker.

Chapter 5:

CELTIC CHRISTIAN SPIRITUALITY: A HOLY EMBRACE OF SPIRIT AND NATURE

The pre-Christian culture in Ireland and other Celtic lands expressed itself in story and image, not written language. Yet, the writings and stories recorded during the Celtic Christian period allow us to glimpse the cultural ambiance into which the Christian message came and gain insight into the way in which the Christian message was received and integrated by the Celts. We begin to see the essential aspects of these earlier cultures that had evolved over time into a cultural climate where the Christian message thrived, eventually creating the golden age of Celtic Christianity.

The Druidic heritage

Although the coming of Christianity to Ireland is shrouded in some degree of mystery, it is believed to have arrived around the first or second century CE. The Ireland into which it arrived was rural and tribal. There were no towns or cities. People would have been identified by the *tuath* or tribe to which they belonged. Druidism, the religion of the people in Celtic lands, had many different ranks within its hierarchy. Priests, shamans, prophets, healers, judges, poets, and bards all had their unique roles and functions.

In this oral spiritual tradition, all subjects were taught through the medium of poetry. A close bond existed between students and teachers during the demanding training required to become a druid. The practise of *anam cara* or soul friend was also central in the Druidic culture. The Druids had an extensive knowledge of the natural world and the laws of nature, which supported their healing abilities and magical ways of knowing.

The connection between the spiritual and the material world, together with a sense of the unbroken wholeness of the universe, underpinned their traditions. They also held a strong belief in the continuity of life after physical death.

The immanence of God

This was the milieu into which the seed of the Christian message was planted, took root, and grew into the unique flowering of Celtic Christianity. How do we understand the essence of that particular expression of the Christian message? While both the Celts and the early Christians accepted and understood the transcendence of God, the Celts emphasized the immanence of God. This belief in God's ubiquitous presence in the world pre-dated the advent of Christianity. Its earliest known Celtic expression is in the poem attributed to Amergin, the Milesean poet believed to have come to Ireland with the first Celtic people. In this poem, Amergin relates the many expressions of the "I am" presence in the manifest world:

I am Wind on Sea,
I am Ocean-wave,
I am Roar of Sea,
I am Bull of Seven Flights,
I am Vulture on Cliff,
I am Dewdrop,
I am Fairest of Flowers,
I am Boar for Boldness,
I am Salmon in Pool,
I am Lake on Plain . . .
I am a Word of Skill,
I am the Point of a Weapon (that poureth forth combat),
I am God who fashioneth Fire for a Head.
Who smootheth the ruggedness of a mountain?
Who is He who announceth the ages of the Moon?
And who, the place where falleth the sunset?[1]

In a more unusual translation of this famous invocation, Amergin speaks of the role of divine energy in the creation of the world and challenges us to develop that discerning eye that can "see" and call forth into our awareness the hidden divine presence:

Who but I am the secret of the dolmen unhewn?
Inside the rocks' bright darkness,
a spark only the blind-to-surfaces can see,
I wait all idea, ideal.
I hide myself in potential to await
the discerning eye and the knowing hand
to lure me forth from
my womb of forever pregnant stone.[2]

For the Celts, the immanence of God also is reflected in the unity of the natural and spiritual worlds, resulting in an intimacy among humanity, the natural world, and divinity. H. J. Massingham in *Tree of Life* describes this belief as "a gleam of a new philosophy of heaven and earth in interdependence and interaction and formulated by a culture in vital contact with the ancient nature-worship."[3] In such a sacramental world, every atom of the created universe contained a spark of divine energy. The animals, plants, fish, birds, insects, the water, the air, the earth itself, and all realms of the universe embodied aspects of divinity. There was no separation into sacred and secular, no division between spirit and matter. The material world emerged from the spiritual world. This is expressed beautifully by Seán Ó Duinn:

Fundamentally all is one and behind this unceasing procession of forms is Dia na nDúl— the God of the elements, earth, fire, water, air, as he was known to the Irish Celts, the God, present, immanent, in the kaleidoscope of life.[4]

Everything was interconnected, the unbroken wholeness pervading everything.

Belief in the omnipresence of God is later reflected in this conversation between St. Patrick and Eithne Alba, a mythological figure representing the old faith present at the time when Christianity arrived in Ireland.

The questions that Eithne Alba poses to St Patrick:
Who is God, and where is God,
Of whom is God, and where His dwelling?
. . . .
Is He ever-living and beautiful?
. . . .
Is He in heaven or on the earth?
In the sea, in the rivers, in the mountains? In the valleys?
Speak to us tidings of Him:
How will He be seen,
How is He loved,
How is He found?

St. Patrick's reply:
Our God is the God of all men [people],
The God of heaven and earth,
The God of the sea and the streams,
The God of sun, moon and stars
. . . .
He has a dwelling in all heaven and earth and sea
And in all things that are in them.

In a further response to Eithne, Patrick emphasises that this divine presence is not passive, but actively engaged in shaping the material, elemental world:

He inspires all things, He quickens all things,
He is over all things, He supports all things.
He makes the light of the sun to shine.[5]

This active divine presence within the elemental world confers on it a power that can be invoked to support and protect people in their daily lives. This belief in the power of the elements to bless and protect is beautifully expressed in the "St. Patrick's Breastplate," also known as the "Deer's Cry," which is believed to have been written after Patrick's time:

I arise today through the strength of heaven:
light of sun, brilliance of moon,
splendour of fire, speed of lightning, swiftness of wind,
depth of the sea, stability of earth, firmness of rock.[6]

This prayer clearly acknowledges the power present in the elements and calls on these forces to bless and protect human beings. It reflects the belief that there is something holy and powerful already present in the natural world—something that is living, vibrant, and responsive, something that has the power to bless and to protect.

Ó Duinn speaks of this living force as *neart*. It is related to what is known as *dabhar* in the Jewish tradition, the *chi* in Taoism, *prana* in Hinduism. This force or *neart* is an expression of the invisible world penetrating the visible world, of spirit penetrating matter. By its presence, this force brings all life into existence; it infuses such presence into all that it creates. This belief is shared by many primal people throughout the world. According to Ó Duinn, the concept of *neart* was first experienced as an impersonal force by the Megalithic people. Later, it was embodied in the archetypal energies expressed in the pantheon of gods and goddesses associated with Celtic people. In the Christian era, it is expressed as Christ-consciousness. This concept is still evolving and has found more recent expression as the noosphere in the writings of Teilhard de Chardin. *Neart* is the creative energy emerging from God, ever present and ever changing, expressing itself in the myriad of shapes and forms that comprise the manifest world.

This divine presence in the physical, material world has been celebrated by many poets over the centuries. Kathleen Raine, in her poem "The Wilderness," speaks of her journey into this dimension of the world:

Yet I have glimpsed the bright mountain
    behind the mountain
Knowledge under the leaves, tasted the bitter
    berries red,
Drunk cold water and clear from an
    inexhaustible hidden fountain.[7]

Patrick Kavanagh, in his poem "Common Beauty," describes the pervasive presence of God: "God's truth was such a thing you could not mention without being ashamed of its commonness."[8] He believes that there is no patch of Monaghan, his home place, that can't also be a patch of Eden. Kavanagh's poetry constantly challenges us to awaken sufficiently that we might see the radiance of the inner world shining through the outer world.

Meditation: Awakening to the "I am" presence within

This meditation, inspired by the words of Amergin above, offers you a pathway into an awareness of the "I am" presence and an opportunity to experience your own unique connection with that presence. You may want to record it or have someone read it aloud to you:

Become aware of your body sitting on your chair, a cushion, or the floor. Notice how your body feels in this moment. Exercise no judgement, just observation. Move your body so that you are comfortable and your body is at ease.

Become aware of your breath, not the thought of your breath, but the actual reality of your breath as it enters and leaves your body in each moment. Notice without judgement how your breath happens from moment to moment, simply observing not judging each breath as it comes and goes. Each breath unique: no holding, no struggling, just your awareness of this breath in this moment.

If your breath is slow, let it be slow. If it is fast, let it be fast. If it is deep, let it be deep. If it is shallow, let it be shallow.

Bringing this attention to your breath allows you to be aware of the subtle changes happening in your breath from moment to moment.

I invite you now to focus your awareness over the next five breaths on your exhalations. With each exhalation, allow yourself to sink deeper and deeper into your core self and into the inner realm of reality deep within you. As you do, you feel yourself connecting with that aspect of yourself that is a part of all that is—a spacious place where there is no holding, no attaching, just the awareness of this moment and the vastness of being. Being present in this place allows you to connect through the breath with all that is, with the vastness of the universe and with the energy and presence that pervades everything. Rest here and spend some time now, allowing your connection with this place to deepen.

And while you rest in this deep place within. I invite you to listen again to these words spoken first by the Celtic poet Amergin:

I am wind over water;
I am a tear the sun lets fall;
I am hawk above the cliff;
I am salmon in pool;
I am boar ruthless and strong;
I am hill where poets walk;
I am spear in battle;
I am wonder among the flowers;
I am! I am! I am! I am! I am! I am!

As you hear these words, pay attention to what it is that stirs within your heart and your soul. Allow yourself to feel your connection with your own "I am" presence, the deep presence that you share with the entire symphony of life. How does this feel? How do you feel as you experience this connection? Bask in this presence for a while longer.

Now slowly bring your awareness back to your breath, to the inhalation and exhalation of your breath. Become aware of your body on the chair, cushion, or floor. Become aware of your feet, your legs, your lower body, your arms, your upper body, your head, and your face. Become aware of yourself reconnecting with the physical realm as you bring your consciousness back into this present moment, to your own self, and your own reality in this place and time. As you gather yourself into your own presence, you carry with you the deep knowing of your connection with all life, through your "I am" presence.

Allow this reality to accompany and support you on your journey today. Whenever you become fearful, angry or disheartened, stop! Bring your attention to your breath, and through the breath become aware again of your connection with your "I am" presence.

Know that in that place of "I am" presence, there is no anger, no fear, no guilt, no shame, no judgement. All that is present in this place is "The 'I am' presence, which is Love."

Know that this is the core of your being; this is the truth of who you are!

Ecology and holiness

A striking and relevant core value present in Celtic Christianity is the connection between ecology and holiness, reflected in a relationship with the natural world that was not sentimental. Rather, this relationship understood both the power and strength of the elements and the paradoxical fragility of the natural world. It was an understanding that the relationship between the people and the land was crucial to the health and well-being of both. This belief, central as it was to Celtic Christianity, had its genesis deep in the ancestral beliefs about the land and its people. It emerged from the pre-Christian love of nature based on the sacredness of the natural world and the continuity between the spiritual and secular worlds. Celtic Christians understood that loving God required a commitment to living in harmony with the natural world. This worldview has been expressed in our day by Thomas Berry, writing in *The Dream of Earth*:

Our fulfilment is not in our isolated human grandeur, but in our intimacy with the larger earth community, for this is also the larger dimension of our being. Our human destiny is integral with the destiny of the earth.[9]

For these Celtic people, the natural world was the ground of their being, the only place where they could have a physical existence. They perceived themselves and their lives to be inextricably linked with the natural world.

Relationship was at the heart of Celtic Christian society and religion. Justice was based on and derived its authority from an appreciation of right relationships, not from legalism. To live well required that one be in right relationship with oneself, with other people, with the earth, with all the worlds, and with the Divine. When right relationship was forfeited or ignored, a breach of justice occurred. Resolving the issue involved an acknowledgement of the breach and taking an action that led to a return to right relationship. People often fasted against the person whom they perceived to be the perpetrator of the injustice, until the situation was resolved. The central role of relationship among Celtic peoples at the time when they encountered Christianity had its origins in the concept of sovereignty, which represents the most fundamental of all relationships.

Sovereignty and the land

What exactly does *sovereignty* mean? Sovereignty is related to the life-giving power of the land, to *neart*, to the fertility of the land itself. It is also related to authority, a word whose root meaning is "to author life." For the Celts and pre-Celtic people, true authority comes from the spirit of sovereignty held within the land, represented as a feminine principle and often named as a particular goddess, who reflected the divine nature held in the land in a specific location.

When a king was chosen to rule, part of his inauguration ceremony was a ritual marriage to the local goddess who represented the sovereignty of the land. It was through this marriage that he could claim his right to rule, his authority. There is, in fact, no word in the Irish language for *inauguration*. The king-ship ritual was known as Bainis Ri or the sacred wedding of the king with the goddess of the land. A similar ritual also existed in ancient civilizations in the Near East and India.[10] This wed-ding symbolically represented the coming together, in an inter-dependent union, of the human world, the natural world, and the unseen world. If the reign of the king was a just one, then the goddess of the land gave forth in abundance. If the king acted unjustly during his rule, then the land withheld its bounty and, consequently, the king's rule was seen as unsuccessful, and he was deemed unfit to remain in the role of king. When his relationship with the sovereignty of the land was compromised, the king lost his authority and his right to rule.

It is important to understand that these earlier Celtic people lived with a deep respect for the natural world not because they were morally superior to us, but because they had a different perception of the world and created their worldview from a dif-ferent story. Their cultural narrative understood the material world as imbued with divinity. It would be foolish to believe that people in times past were perfect and always lived up to the ideals of their culture or religion. What we can take away from the early Celtic Christians, however, is an understanding of reality and a set of ideals that we recognise today as deeply ecological. Central to the lives of these people was their quest to understand their place within the universe. They also were acutely aware of the divine presence immanent in all aspects of the world—including in human life. Advancing in holiness, which is the aim of all spiritual journeys, involved for them an effort to develop this awareness of the presence of God in eve-rything and everybody, above us, below us, and all around us at the four points of the compass.[11]

The two pillars of Celtic Christianity

The accounts and stories from the early Christian period in Ireland and the British Isles give us a glimpse into that world. The Celtic monks and saints saw nature and scripture as the two shoes of Christ. Their daily lives combined scholarly scriptural reflective work and the physical effort of cultivating the earth in ways that reflected their gentle love for their fellow creatures and all creation. This is related in the many wonderful stories and legends from the lives of the Celtic saints shared by Shirley Toulsen and Christopher Bamford. The following stories reflect the close affinity between animals and humans and give the sense of these connections. We begin with the tale of St. Kevin in Glendalough:

> Even though it was an angel who urged Kevin to cultivate the wild slopes of the Wicklow hills, he declined the suggestion. "I have no wish that the creatures of God should be moved because of me. . . . My God can help that place in some other fashion. And, moreover, all the wild creatures on these mountains are my housemates, gentle and familiar with me, and they would be sad of this that thou has said."[12]

Another story tells of St. Cuthbert attempting to be self-sufficient in his monastery. Birds came and perched on his spouting barley:

> Instead of throwing stones at them or scaring them off, he spoke gently to them saying, "Why are you touching a crop that you did not sow? Or is it that you have more need of it than I? If you have God's leave, do what he allows you: but if not, be off, and do no more damage to what is not your own." The biographer tells us that the birds flew off and never trespassed on the crop again.[13]

A horse was reputed to have found food from under a thatch roof for St. Cuthbert, while sea otters dried and warmed him after he had spend the night praying and chanting in the sea.

Other stories tell of how the saints trusted the animals to show them the correct place for their monasteries. St. Gobnat founded her monastery at Ballyvourney in County Cork where she saw nine white deer; this was the sign she had be given to indicate the location of her monastery. Ciaran of Clonmacnoise was led to his place by a stag. Following the animals also had a practical dimension, because the animals would choose a place convenient to a water source.[14] These stories of monastic settlements provide another example of the intersection between the physical and spiritual worlds of the Celt.

The early saints also had an intimate knowledge of the healing properties of plants and herbs, knowledge that they may have inherited from the Druidic teachings. Healings done with these plants were common and often resulted in seemingly miraculous cures.

The saints' relationship with the plant and animal worlds was finely tuned through intense spiritual practice. These accounts suggest a people whose spirituality was rooted in the natural world and yet who had the capacity to see through nature into the spiritual world. Robin Flower, writing about the monks of the early Christian church, says,

> It was not only that these scribes and anchorites lived by the destiny of their dedication in an environment of wood and sea; it was because they brought into that environment an eye washed miraculously clear by continuous spiritual exercise that they, first in Europe, had that strange vision of natural things in an almost unnatural purity.[15]

Their spiritual exercises, I believe, would have involved meditation and learning to see, hear, smell, touch, and taste in a fully conscious way. The Gaelic word for meditation is *rinnfheitheamh*, which literally means point-waiting or point-watching.[16] Such practices would counteract any tendency toward inattentiveness, half-seeing, or half-hearing and build the ability to be completely present in the moment with full attention. Devotees would gain the capacity to see into the heart and soul of everything, using the highly developed skills of imagination—a gift from the pre-Christian Celts—that allowed them to enter the non-material, yet real, inner world where spirit resides.

Enough is plenty

As in all life situations, a difference exists between the ideal and the ability of humans to live up to that ideal. The Celtic Christians took seriously the promise in Deuteronomy that those who love God will have plentiful crops and good pasture for their cattle[17], which in practical terms, required people to express their love of God by taking care of their own piece of the earth and living with respect for all of God's creation. They understood that the opposite of love was greed, not hate—greed that arose from a lack of reverence for creation, a lack of trust, and ignorance of one's true place in the world.

Several stories from the early Christian times show how the harmony with nature could be disrupted when people became selfish and broke the bonds of right relationship. In the following story, we can see clearly the result of breaking away from harmonious relationship with the earth:

> Once all of the saints in Ireland came to Columba's Durrow to fast against God. They were furious with the Almighty because the penitents, whom they had put on bread and water to make reparation for their sins, all died. An angel came to rebuke the saints at their anger at what seemed to be a divine injustice. "Wonder not if the bread and water cannot sustain the penitents today," said the heavenly messenger. "The fruits and the plants of the earth have been devastated, so that there is neither strength nor force in them to support anyone. The falsehood and sin and injustice of men have robbed the earth with its fruits of their strength and force. When men were obedient to God's will the plants of the earth retained their proper strength. At that time water was no worse for sustaining people than milk is today."[18]

This story certainly has relevance in our present world, as does another that challenges the assumed benefits of the over-consumption of resources. The tale relates the disapproval of Neot, a saint who lived in Britain, at the wasteful overuse of resources:

This holy man had a pool by his settlement in which three
fish swam. Every day he ate one fish, and every morning there
were still three fish swimming. One day the saint fell sick and
did not feel like eating anything at all. Still the three fish went
on swimming in the pool. Eventually Neot's companions,
hoping to tempt the saint to eat by offering a choice of dishes,
cooked each fish in a different manner. When the saint saw
what food was spread before him, he was aghast. Immediately
he recovered sufficiently to order the three untouched dishes
to be emptied into the water. At once the fish returned to life
and swam away. Now restored to health, Neot went back to
his practice of eating one of the inexhaustible supply each
day.[19]

This story clearly links the wise use of resources with the
ability to create a sustainable living situation at the saint's settlement. The saint understands the connection between abundance and a sense of gratitude and reverence for the source and
supply of food, together with an appropriate use of resources.
This reflects an attitude so utterly different from the current
western belief system where abundance is seen as endless, leading to senseless consumerism.

The ebbing of Celtic Christianity

This world of the Celtic Christian settlement or monastery,
with its saint and his or her followers, was the distinctive form
of the Celtic church and continued to be the dominant type
of Christianity in both Ireland and the British Isles until the
Synod of Whitby (England) in 664 CE. At Whitby, the growing tensions between the Celtic Christian churches and the
church based in Rome came to a head, and the Roman form
of Christianity began to take precedence over the Celtic church
in England. The Celtic church remained the dominant form of
Christianity in Wales and Scotland for at least another hundred
years, and in Ireland, the Celtic church survived as a unique
entity until the ninth or tenth century. However, after the Synod
of Whitby, "we lost a form of individual Christianity which,

through its druidic roots, was truly linked to the perennial philosophy of humanity."[20]

The demise of the Celtic church was a significant loss to the development of western culture. According to H. J. Massingham, "if the British [Celtic] Church had survived, it is possible that the fissure between Christianity and nature, widening through the centuries, would not have cracked the unity of western man's attitude to the universe."[21]

What is both surprising and wonderful is the extent to which this spiritual tradition survived on the margins of the Celtic world—on the western shores of Wales and Scotland and especially in the rural parts of Ireland. Because of the amazing work of Alexander Carmichael in gathering the prayers, blessings, and stories from people in the highlands and the islands of Scotland and that of Douglas Hyde in rural Ireland, much of this rich and unique spiritual tradition has been preserved for posterity. When we explore some of these prayers and blessings, we are drawn into the magical, spirit-filled world of our Celtic ancestors. These prayers of ordinary people give us a sense of the fabric and colour of the landscape and mindset inhabited by these people—where they lived, loved, fought, gave birth, and died. It is from this rich source that we may, if we are willing, be able to receive the spiritual nourishment that will light the way forward for us in the wasteland created by the present materialistic society.

Prayer in everyday life

Seán Ó Duinn reflects how prayers and rituals were used to build up an awareness of God, so that a person's daily life became the vehicle for becoming both aware of and united with God.[22] The many different tasks and situations that reflected daily and yearly experience each had their own prayers, whose repetition expanded the energy available to support the person performing the particular task.

The Consecration of the Seed
>   I will go out to sow the seed,
>   In name of Him who gave it growth;
>
>   . . . .
>
>   I will come round with my step,
>   I will go rightways with the sun.
>
>   . . . .
>
>   Be giving growth and kindly substance
>   To every thing that is in my ground .[23]

Those who speak the above prayer understand that it is their job is to sow the seed and invoke blessings on it. They also know that the gift of growth comes from somewhere else, from the dimension where the creative energy or *neart* resides.

In this milking blessing, we experience the mutual partnership shared among the cow, its owner, and the Divine:

>   Bless, O God, my little cow,
>   Bless, O God, my desire;
>   Bless Thou my partnership
>   And the milking of my hands, O God.
>
>   . . . .
>
>   Give the milk, my treasure!
>
>   . . . .
>
>   Give the milk
>   And thou'lt get a reward:
>   Grasses of the plains.
>
>   . . . .
>
>   Give the milk,
>   And thou'lt have the blessing
>   Of the King of the earth.[24]

Many of the prayers celebrate the sense of cosmic connection that people experienced more fully in times past. The sun and the moon were frequent subjects for praise.

New Moon
 There, see, the new moon,
 The King of life blessing her;
 Fragrant be every night
 Whereon she shall shine!

 . . . .

 Be her light above
 With every one in straits;
 Be her guidance below
 With every one in need.[25]

Sun
 The eye of the great God,
 . . . .
 The eye of the King of the living,
 Pouring upon us
 At each time and season,
 Pouring upon us
 Gently and generously.

 Glory to thee,
 Thou glorious sun.

 Glory to thee, thou sun,
 Face of the God of life.[26]

God's protection was invoked at all new beginnings, as reflected in the following two prayers:

The journey prayer
> O God, bless every step
> That I am taking,
> And bless the ground
> Beneath my feet.
> Bless to me, O God,
> the path whereon I go;
> Bless to me, O God,
> the thing of my desire.[27]

The blessing for a new home
> A blessing upon your new home,
> A blessing upon your new hearth,
> A blessing upon your new dwelling,
> Upon your newly kindled fire.[28]

I find the following prayer particularly beautiful and wonder what might result from invoking it when a young person today sets out on his or her own:

Blessing for a young person leaving home
> We bathe your palms in showers of wine,
> In the crook of the kindling, in the seven elements,
> In the sap of the tree, in the milk of honey.
> We place nine pure, choice gifts
> In your clear beloved face:
> The gift of form, the gift of voice,
> The gift of fortune, the gift of goodness,
> The gift of eminence, the gift of charity,
> The gift of integrity, the gift of true nobility,
> The gift of apt speech.[29]

In the following prayer, one gets a sense of openness to the possibilities that may arise during the day:

Blessing before leaving home for work
    This day is your love gift to me.
    This dawn . . . I take it from your hands.
    Make me busy in your service throughout its hours,
    yet not so busy that I cannot sing a happy song.[30]

Yet then as now, we may experience disappointment with
how we are and where our lives are going, as the following
prayer so compassionately expresses:

Blessing in dissatisfaction
    Many a time I wish I were other than I am.
    I weary of the solemn tide;
        of little fields;
            of this brooding isle.

    I long to be rid of the weight of duty
    and to have my part in ampler life.
    O Thou, who art wisdom and pity both,
    set me free from the lordship of desire.

    Help me to find my happiness
    in my acceptance of what is my purpose:
    in friendly eyes;
        in work well done;
            in quietness born of trust,
                and, most of all,
    in the awareness of your presence in my spirit. [31]

A common form of prayer was the *lúireach*, the protection prayer, the best known of which is the "Breastplate of St. Patrick," discussed earlier in this chapter. This prayer calls on the elements, the communion of saints, all the aspects of divinity for protection:

> I arise today through the strength of heaven,
> Light of sun, radiance of moon.
>
> . . . .
>
> I arise today
> Through a mighty strength, the invocation of the trinity,
> Through belief in the threeness,
> Through the confession of the oneness
> Of the creator of creation.[32]

All of these prayers from the Celtic Christian tradition, whether they were composed recently or in the distant past, contain ancient ideas and patterns of thought. They celebrate the concept of blessing—blessing as the consecration and mingling of the mundane with the sacred in a way that confers grace and protection. Within these prayers lies an ancient pattern of thought that reflects essential ideas about life and God, the thread of an enduring belief in the unity of the cosmos in which the material and spiritual worlds flow into and out of each other in a natural and unselfconscious way.

Chapter 6

THE DIVINE FEMININE IN
CELTIC SPIRITUALITY

" God is good, and he has a great mother!" This statement, sometimes heard in Ireland, reflects an important truth at the heart of the Celtic spiritual tradition, one that honours the presence of the divine feminine and understands that even God emerges out of the feminine energy of being-ness. The presence of the divine feminine is central in both the Celtic spiritual tradition and culture.

The divine feminine has three different, but related manifestations—the maiden, the mother, and the *cailleach*, or crone—which together comprise a feminine trinity. Each aspect of this trinity occupies a different role within the life, death, and rebirth continuum, another central concept in Celtic cosmology.

Both masculine and feminine energies are fully embraced in this tradition. Both are understood as central to manifestation on this physical plane. All aspects of life, death, and rebirth result from interactions between the masculine and feminine energies, which are honoured through the pantheon of gods and goddesses that inhabit the pre-Christian Celtic myths and legends. Some of these gods and goddesses have been subsumed into Christian faith and are embodied in the saints, thus ensuring the ongoing presence of this energy in the world.

Brigid, goddess and saint

Of all these archetypal figures, Brigid as both goddess and saint occupies a central place within Celtic consciousness. Her presence was already very strong in the hearts, minds, and psyches of the people at the time of the arrival of Christianity. This ensured her continued and undiluted role in the spiritual life of the people, especially in Ireland. Many of the qualities and attributes of the pre-Christian goddess Brigid were later associated with the woman who founded the abbey in Kildare in the sixth century CE.

As a goddess, Brigid was associated with poetry, learning, healing, and smithcraft and also with fertility and new life. Celtic scholar Proinsias Mac Cana says,

> Paradoxically, it is in the person of her Christian namesake St. Brigid that the pagan goddess survives best. For if the historical element in the legend of St. Brigid is slight, the mythological element is correspondingly extensive, and it is clear beyond question that the saint has usurped the role of the goddess and much of her mythological tradition. . . . It must be accepted that no clear distinction can be made between the goddess and the saint and that in all probability Brigid's great monastery of Kildare was formerly a pagan sanctuary.[1]

Pádraigín Clancy refers to the understanding that St. Brigid has power to control the nature kingdoms, that she is endowed with extraordinary miraculous powers, and that her monastery was a place of refuge, healing, and justice for all pilgrims. She believes that the saint embodies much of the lore of the previous Goddess tradition and that these two strands link us into the story of the eternal feminine within Celtic spirituality.[2] In the Celtic Christian tradition, St. Brigid was and still is a central embodiment of the divine feminine and is closely associated with Mary, the mother of Jesus; she is often known in Ireland as *Mhuire na Gael* (Mary of the Irish).

How can we recognise the divine feminine? What qualities comprise its archetypal energy? Feminine energy is both the harbinger and the birther of new life and the destroyer of life that has been spent. Existing as it does in three forms—the maiden, the mother, and the crone—it is present at the thresholds of life and death and rebirth.

Brigid, although normally associated with the maiden and mother aspects of feminine energy, is also expressed in the *cailleach* form, as indicated in the prayer "*Molamid Brid an mhaighean; Molamid Brid an mhathair; Molamid Brid an cailleach*" (Praise to Brigid, the maiden, the mother, and the crone). In this context, Brigid may refer to an even older goddess archetype.

The name Brigid comes from the word *brig*, which means exalted one or high one and is associated with power and authority. Alexi Kondratiev comments that in some Celtic languages the word *brig* suggests "force, power, meaning, invigorating essence" and is, therefore, associated with an archetypal energy rather than an individual person.[3]

Brigid of Kildare and her congregation are often associated or compared with the vestal virgins who played a vital symbolic role in Roman culture. The two main functions of the consecrated virgins in both Rome and Kildare were to tend the sacred fire and to ensure the state of virginity of the women themselves. This particular concept of virginity had a wider meaning beyond the absence of sexual activity: The vestal virgins were a symbol of the unity of culture. Each of these virgins represented a person who was whole unto herself and could maintain her unity and integrity, without it being compromised by another person. Such a state of virginity was developed through intense spiritual and psychological practices. Its potency was central to the well-being of the tribe or society, because while virginal, it held within it the capacity to bring forth new life. This virginity thus represented a source of fertility and fecundity within the state and its institutions.

Seán Ó Duinn has traced the distinct pattern that emerges with similarities in the archetypal idea of the perpetual fire tended in Kildare and Rome, each by 20 virgins. In both cases, oak was the wood burned in the fires, and men were excluded from the fire enclosure. The circular enclosure was made from hedges in Kildare, while in Rome the fire was contained in a circular temple.[4]

The elemental fire energy that plays an important role in the mythology of Brigid, both as goddess and saint, was understood to have both destructive and constructive aspects. In Kildare, the sacred fire of Brigid was seen as central to the life and work of the abbey and its community, where it was tended by the nuns and was kept alight for more than 700 years. In

1993, the Brigid fire was re-kindled by the Brigidine Sisters in Kildare, and the flame now burns perpetually in Solas Bhride and in the centre of Kildare town.[5] In 2009, members of Brat Bhride Dundalk brought the flame from Kildare to Faughart, County Louth, the birthplace of Brigid.[6]

The life-enhancing fire of Brigid would not burn or destroy a person so long as that individual maintained integrity and stayed clearly focused on his or her intention. This fire was the life-force within, the power to create, to sustain, and to enhance new life in all its manifestations. In the following story, Mary Condren illustrates one of the important roles of fire within Brigid's monastery:

> Fire was also the means through which Brigit knew if her nuns had been faithful. Every morning, one of her nuns, Darlughdacha, . . . went to collect the seed of the fire. On one unfortunate morning, when she returned, the fire had burned through her apron, symbolising that her purity had been compromised. Shamefully, she confessed to Brigit that indeed a blacksmith had admired her ankles. Brigit told her to put coals in her shoes to purify herself once again, and Darlughdacha eventually became her successor in Kildare.[7]

Fire here is used as a purification ritual, perhaps similar to the fire-walking ceremony found in other cultures. Symbolically, the purity in the story of Darlughdacha is that of intention. Its loss would have compromised her capacity to be virginal, in the sense of being a person whole unto herself, undivided. She and Brigid's other followers were charged with holding the seed of the fire on behalf of the community—that is, guarding the seeds of a life-enhancing energy on behalf of the people. This fire would not burn or be destructive so long as the virgins remained focused, aligned with their own inner truth, and undistracted by flattery or popular opinions. So, for we who are charged with embodying the energy of Brigid today, it is essential that we stay focused on our task, which is to act, like Brigid, as midwives to a new era, a new day, a new way of being in the world.

The literature about Brigid, who remains the key manifestation of the divine feminine in Ireland, also highlights her many attributes related to her generativity: her capacity to bring forth new life, to nourish, to create plenty in the crops or an abundance of the milk from cows, and to manifest or create *ex nihilo*. Brigid is strongly associated with true abundance and with the prosperity of the society, living in relationship with the land. Energetically, she represents the goddess of sovereignty, the life-giving *neart* or life force.

The stories of the miracles attributed to her during her Christian phase mirror the qualities that were present in the pre-Christian manifestation of the goddess Brigid. Many of the miracles recorded in Cogitosus' *Life of St. Brigid* relate to her kindness and generosity and to her ability to manifest abundantly all that was needed in each moment. She had the capacity to restore that which she had given away, as in the story of the bacon that she gave to a hungry dog and then had it reappear in time for dinner and the story that tells of her giving away milk and butter and yet the same amount remaining. Another story tells of her ability to control the natural world and relates how she stopped the rain in her locality to allow the corn to be harvested. Other stories show her deep compassion for the human condition as when, for example, she prayed and removed the pain of childbirth from a young woman as she gave birth.[8]

Brigid is a threshold person who can straddle both sides and remain detached. This quality, which is central in her life, is highlighted in the stories of her birth, which attest that she was born on the threshold of the house, neither within nor without; that her father was a noble man, her mother a slave; and that he was a pagan, her mother a Christian. From her origins, she has this ability to stand in the void and remain centred within it, while holding the creative tension between two opposite perspectives. Many stories from her life portray her as a person capable of resolving conflicts in a healthy manner. Being centred and aligned within herself, she can grasp the energies of both sides clearly and so can facilitate a resolution. She has the ability to stand still and remain focused, in spite of the uncertainty present in the outer world. Each of us can and must develop this quality of being centred and aligned with one's deep inner knowing, in order to further the creation of a new society.

It is reputed that from the time when she learned to know God, her mind remained ever focused on God. She remained connected to God and the heavens while living on the earthly plane. Her power of manifestation was a result of this ability to be aligned heaven to earth and to connect her inner and outer worlds, thus focusing energy onto a particular intention and ensuring its manifestation. The story of St. Brendan and the whale reflects the alignment of heaven and earth within Brigid and the power that flows through her because of that alignment:

> One day, he was standing on a cliff looking out to sea and suddenly two whales jumped out of the water and began to fight. A great battle takes place and gradually the smaller whale is getting weaker and St. Brendan sees that it is only a matter of time before the bigger whale kills him. But just as he is about to be killed the smaller whale shouts out with a human voice calling on St. Brigit to save him. And with that, the big whale goes away leaving the small whale unharmed. Now, St. Brendan was watching all this and he because very upset. He said to himself: "Why did the whale call on Brigit to save him and not on me? . . . . The whales all know me and are used to seeing me on the sea; they all know that I am a holy man and that I can get whatever I want from God. Why did the whale ignore me and call on Brigit?". . . .
>
> St. Brendan could find no answer to this question so he decided that the only thing to do was to ask Brigit herself for an explanation. . . .
>
> When St. Brendan met St. Brigit, he told her what had happened and asked her to explain why the whale had considered her to be a greater saint than himself and had ignored him even though he was actually on the spot when the incident occurred. . . . "Tell me," says St. Brigit, "is your mind constantly on God; are you constantly aware of him?" "Well," says St. Brendan, "I am generally aware of God, but I live a very busy

and dangerous life. Often the sea is very rough and storms arise and on these occasions I forget all about God as I am so preoccupied trying to keep afloat." "That is the explanation," says Brigit, "for since the first day I set my mind on God I have never taken it away from him and I never will."⁹

In other words, she never faltered in her awareness of God's presence. Moreover, she was able to contemplate both God and an earthly goal and thus accomplish whatever she set her mind upon in this world. Many contemporary teachings about the laws of attraction and laws of manifestation are a modern version of Brigid's attentiveness. A new awareness of this power features in the work of Gerry and Esther Hicks and their many books on the subject.¹⁰

The role of the divine feminine in today's world

When we look at the dominant forces in our world today, focused as they are on manipulation of the earth, its resources, and its people, we see that many of these forces are in direct conflict with the ideals of a life-enhancing society, which would be one created by considering the needs, not only of all humans, but of the whole earth community. The worldview adopted by a life-enhancing society would be reflected in the ethos and practices of the institutions that served that society. The founding ideologies of these institutions would reflect the true nature of the world we inhabit. Such a worldview would understand that human beings emerge from the natural world, are defined by their relationships within the natural world, and that they can live successfully only where healthy relationships with the natural environment are maintained. Such a society would honour the age-old wisdom that understands the earth as sacred and acknowledges the divine feminine energy present within the landscape, embodied by the goddesses of ancient times. It would understand that to honour the goddess is to live in right relationship with the land.

Such a society would honour the sovereignty of the land, that most ancient, life-giving aspect of the land, ensuring prosperity for the tribe, because it would know that if the sovereignty was compromised, the harvest would fail. The king would be deemed to have breached the laws of right relationship with the land goddess and would have to resign. However, today's patriarchal society has no understanding of either the goddess, the divine feminine, or of the sacredness of the earth. We live in a society that understands little about meaningful relationships with the earth or with the many non-human species with which we share this planet. Our present way of living is creating a wasteland, not only of the earth, but within the human heart and human soul. Living in this spiritual wasteland further limits our ability to interact in a meaningful way with the natural world. This results in a society that is out of touch with its mother, the earth, and so we are like motherless children, searching everywhere for a sense of relatedness and for a sense of home.

Hope for the future

Is there any cause for hope, or is there any possibility that we, as a society, can recover from this wasteland that we have created? I believe that there is a way back from this place of destruction. I believe that the archetypal energy of Brigid—the embodiment of the divine feminine present within the essence of the Celtic culture—has the capacity to lead us from death to life and from war to peace, within ourselves and the world. For this to happen, it is necessary for us to understand that the archetypal energy that Brigid represents is an aspect of the human psyche that has been largely dormant over the past few hundred years but is now ready to re-emerge. And it is we who must begin to awaken this Brigid energy present within ourselves so that she can help us to courageously and safely face the demons of this time and be our agent of transformation, the one who can breathe life into the mouth of dead winter as it is expressed in the soulless wasteland at the heart of western society.

However, before this transformation can happen, we must first embrace the energy of the hag or the *cailleach*, which is that dark aspect of the divine feminine associated with death and destruction. We must acknowledge the dark place our society presently inhabits. We must place ourselves, individually and as a society, in the hands of the wise, but challenging energy of the *cailleach*, the death and destroying aspect of the divine feminine energy that will ultimately lead us to a rich and abundant new life.

What then is the energy associated with the hag, crone, or *cailleach* aspect of the divine feminine? The *cailleach* is the embodiment of the tough mother-love that challenges its children to stop acting in destructive ways. It is the energy that refuses to indulge in inappropriate personal or societal dreams. It is the energy that will bring death to those dreams and fantasies that are not aligned with our highest good. Yet, this *cailleach* energy also will support the emergence and manifestation in the world of the highest and deepest within us. It will hold us safely as we embrace the darkness within ourselves and our society. It is an energy that insists that we stand still, open our hearts, and feel our own pain and the pain of the earth. This is the energy that teaches us how to stay with the process when things are difficult. This energy will not allow us to run away!

The great heroes and heroines of all mythologies must face and embrace the *cailleach* energy of surrender, darkness, and death. In so doing, they find their path of action, their true masculine power, which can emerge only when the journey into and through the darkness—represented by the *cailleach* energy—is undertaken. The hero or heroine learns the next step required in the outer world only by submitting to the *cailleach* and her way of being with its slow, inwardly focused activity, its times of waiting, and paying attention. Would that we had any true heroes or heroines leading our world! In order for us to be healed as a society, each of us must embrace this *cailleach* energy and answer the call to be today's great heroes and heroines.

One of the stories from the Celtic tradition that illustrates the importance of the *cailleach* and her energy is the story of Niall of the Nine Hostages. Niall and his four brothers come to a well to get a drink of water. The well is being guarded by an old woman who represents the *cailleach* or hag. When the first brother goes to the well, she tells him that if he wants to drink the water, he must give her a kiss, he is horrified and refuses; she sends him away. The other three brothers go in turn on the same errand, and each refuses to kiss the hag. As the story goes:

> Then it was Niall's turn. Faced with the same challenge, he kissed the old hag and embraced her. When he looked again, she had changed into the most beautiful woman in the world. "What art thou?" said the boy. "King of Tara, I am Sovereignty . . . your seed shall be over every clan."[11]

My understanding of this story is that in order to have access to the life-enhancing energy represented by the water and the well, it is necessary for the young masculine to embrace this particular and perhaps unattractive aspect of the feminine energy. Why is this so? The hag represents the wisdom gathered by living in right relationship with the earth, something that requires reflection, stillness, and attentiveness. It knows more clearly what is needed and what is possible in each situation, and it is aware of the consequences of particular actions. It knows how to proceed slowly; it understands the value of times of waiting and times of allowing. It knows how to be and how to act.

The young masculine energy, with its "can do" attitude—present in both men and women and currently dominating western society—needs to be tempered by embracing the wisdom of the *cailleach*. When this happens, the masculine energy matures and acts in ways that create new life, vitality, and sustainability. The masculine energy learns how to act in the service of the mature feminine, bringing forth wisdom and compassion. Here again, we see the Celtic tradition providing a source of inspiration and hope for our present situation. So often this immature masculine energy, which is impulsive and short-sighted and which does not consider fully the consequences of its actions, dominates in western society. The present ecological and spiritual crisis has resulted largely from the use of this impulsive masculine energy disconnected from its feminine counterpart.

So how can we, you and I, begin the journey back towards wholeness and balance? One idea that may support us is that change is possible only through acceptance of what is in this moment. Thus, every moment holds the possibility for change! The first step is for us to confront the denial, rampant in our culture, about the future consequences of the endless consumerism that is now considered normal in the western global economy. We must be willing to awaken to the part of us that instinctively knows there is something wrong with the number of species made extinct each year, with the destruction of the biodiversity, with massive deforestation, over-fishing of the seas, and pollution of the air and the waters. How can we open ourselves to experience the grief that is held beneath the layers of denial, as we contemplate these vast losses and their consequences for the future of life on this planet?

Brigid in her *cailleach* form can help us to embrace these difficult and fearful aspects of our lives. The cauldron, a central image in both the Celtic and other traditions, is a vessel for transformation and transmutation. In many stories, the cauldron is first filled with unpalatable raw things, which then are used to create a nourishing soup using the transforming energy of the universe through the action of fire and water. The transformation of the contents of the cauldron is supervised by the *cailleach* energy, which works inwardly, quietly, and slowly to bring about an unforced and timely rebirth. The transformation of the cauldron's contents concentrates their essence and offers them back in a new and more suitable form.

From this process, we learn that the possibility of transformation and re-birth always exists, no matter how devitalised something appears to be. A new rebirth can be achieved when we submit ourselves and our concerns to the inward and slow transformational energy of the cauldron and the *cailleach*.[12] This, I believe, is a key for us, both personally and as a society, at this time. Not only can this energy help us to break through the massive denial so prevalent today and embrace the grief that lies beneath the denial, but it also has the capacity to stop the "business as usual" syndrome that keeps us citizens trapped and disempowered. Feeling the grief and sense of loss will lead us to ask deeper questions about the way we live and make meaning of our lives. An Irish *seanfocal* (proverb) assures us that "the key to all knowledge is questioning." The crucial questions will reveal themselves while we are in that quiet inward space in the womb of the dark goddess energy. Asking those crucial questions will show the necessary next steps and offer us a pathway out of our current cultural wasteland. Making choices in our lives from this place of deep reflection will empower each of us to become agents of transformation and to act decisively within our own sphere of influence.

Reclaiming the power of the feminine

What is most needed now on our planet is the strong and clear presence of the feminine energy in all its manifestations. This energy is present and available in different ways to both men and women, although the past few thousand years of patriarchal culture has damaged the ability of both men and women to access and value the feminine, resulting in a distortion of both the true feminine and masculine energies. Women, in particular, need to reconnect with their true feminine energy, embrace it fully, and allow it to influence their daily lives. The Russian mystic Helena Roerich maintained that the most important task for women was to raise their own consciousness and to bring with them the men who were their eternal companions. In 1937, she said:

> Cosmos affirms the greatness of woman's creative principle. Woman is the personification of nature, and it is nature that teaches man, not man nature. Therefore, may all women realize the grandeur of their origins, and may they strive for knowledge. Where there is knowledge there is power.[13]

That women should reclaim their true feminine energy and power is still an urgent task today. In doing so, they will open the way for men to honour the feminine within themselves and within the world. Brigid, as the representative of the divine feminine in the Celtic tradition, will empower each of us to reclaim that feminine energy in all its aspects and to become agents of transformation in our troubled world. The stories of Brigid reflect her many qualities that we need today—courage, compassion, radical personal freedom, generosity, deep connection with the land, ability to resolve conflict, and focused awareness.

Each of us holds the archetypal energy of Brigid deep within. Our task now is to make a personal connection with the energy of Brigid and begin to bring forth the qualities that she embodies in our own lives. It is only in us, you and me, that the energy of Brigid will rise again, take form, and become a force for transformation in our world. These contemporary song lyrics encourage us to believe that the energy and wisdom of Brigid is with us again, reappearing little by little in the world today:

Brighid of the sunrise, rising in the morning,
Rising with the springtime, greening all the land.
See you in the soft cloud; see you in the raindrop;
See you in the winds of change, blowing through the land.
You, the red-eared white cow, nourishing the people,
Nourish now the hunger, soul's longing in our land.
Bird that is unfolding, now the time's upon us.
Only have we eyes to see Your Epiphany.[14]

Meditation with the divine feminine

As a first step toward reconnecting with the life-giving energy of the divine feminine, you may want to engage in the following meditation:

Become aware of your body standing or sitting. Become aware of the space around you.

Become aware of your breath, not the thought of your breath, but the actual experience of your breath as it comes into your body and as it leaves your body. Stay focused on your breath for a few moments. With each exhalation, allow yourself to let go a little more. Allow yourself to surrender to the flow with each exhalation, bringing you deeper into the centre of your own being.

Now bring your awareness to your feet. See, feel, or know that there are cords emerging from the soles of your feet that go deep into the centre of the earth. Take a few moments to experience this connection with the earth. Pause here for a while.

Bring your attention and awareness to your own understanding of the divine feminine energy. Allow yourself to become more and more aware of this energy—aware of how it feels, how it expresses itself within your experience in each moment. Using any or all of your senses, allow an image to emerge that expresses or represents this energy of the divine feminine for you.

Take some time now to be with and to engage with this image.

Pause, and as you rest here, perhaps a question arises or you ponder some issue that needs more insight. Whatever it is that arises within you, allow yourself to be with it in this deep feminine space. Allow this energy to feed you, to nourish you as you wait for a new awareness or a new insight or perhaps even an answer.

Pause, and accept with gratitude whatever gifts you receive here.

Slowly begin to bring yourself back from that deep place within, slowly becoming aware of your breath as it ebbs and flows, slowly becoming aware of your body sitting or standing while still aware of your connection with the deep feminine energy at the centre of the earth and with all existence. Bring your awareness fully back to yourself in this present moment.

When you are ready, open your eyes and stretch.

You may wish to write about insights received in your journal.

Chapter 7:

THE CELTIC YEAR CALENDAR

It would seem that we who live in western society have lost our connection with the rhythm of the cosmos and lost our sense of place within the universe. We experience ourselves as rudderless and disconnected from the larger reality of life and our journey within it. From within the extremely small part of this vast universe that we inhabit, we pay little attention to the cosmic drama that is played out every day and night, absorbed as we are in the minuteness of the worlds to which we give our attention. We fail to notice the subtle and large changes that are constantly happening in our worlds.

We experience time only in a linear way, emerging from the past and heading towards the future. We are always moving either away from the past or towards the future and thus are seldom fully in the present moment. All aspects of time are seen as the same; there are no special moments. In western consciousness, this linear understanding of time is seen as normal and the only way to experience time.

Yet it was not always so, nor is it the case in all societies at present. Many primal and tribal peoples experienced time in a circular and non-linear fashion. This created a different reality within their societies, where time flowed rather than ran always forward. Some traditional cultures still inhabit time in this way.

Different patterns of time

The Celtic and pre-Celtic cultures understood time as seasons of energy that flow into and out of each other in a circular and spiral way. Using this understanding of time, they created a calendar that reflected these seasons and the cosmological events that gave rise to them. The peoples who created and lived by this calendar understood life as an alternation of opposing forces—night and day, winter and summer, darkness and light—that constantly interacted with each other.

In their cosmology, Samhain, at the beginning of winter and the dark season, was the beginning of the new year. They measured time from night to night rather than day to day, because for them night preceded day, as winter preceded summer. These choices stemmed from a fundamental belief that primordial chaos precedes the creation of the cosmos and that gestation, which is always in darkness, precedes birth. Darkness was also present at the end of a process with its dissolution. So for these people, endings and beginnings were intimately connected, as is so beautifully reflected in the wonderful flowing lines and connected figures ubiquitous in Celtic art.

The Celtic year

The Celtic year is divided into two major phases—the *giamos* time, associated with the darkness and winter, and the *samos* time, associated with brightness and summer. The *giamos* time is related to the feminine principle and the realm of the goddess, while the *samos* time is related to the masculine principle and the realm of the god. During the *giamos* time, the non-doing mode of being and the qualities of receptivity and non-linear time are valued. Here, the slow non-rational intuitive ways are dominant. In the *samos* time, outer activity and doing are essential, and operations are carried out in a linear, analytical, and rational way.

The year is further divided into eight sections, or seasons, each having its own unique energy, rhythm, and festival. The four principal festivals of the Celtic year calendar are Samhain, (November 1), Imbolc (February 1), Bealtaine (May 1), and Lughnasadh (August 1), sometimes known as the earth festivals. They correspond to the four significant agricultural festivals of the year and also have connections with the different phases of the moon. The other four festivals are the winter and summer solstices, together with the spring and autumn equinoxes; these mark the significant moments of the earth's journey around the sun.

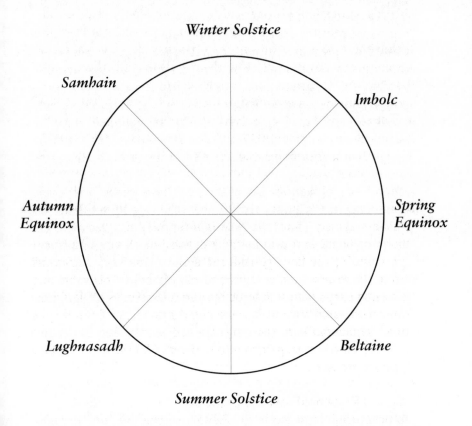

Figure 1
Festivals of the Celtic year

The sun festivals are considered to be masculine, while the festivals associated with agriculture and the moon are considered to be feminine, thus ensuring a balance of both energies within the calendar. The sun festivals may be older than the agricultural festivals, reflecting the rituals of an earlier people that became integrated into the later cultures.

Each sun festival is related to the earth festival that precedes it: The sun festival is considered to express the apex or completion of the energy initiated in the preceding earth festival. Thus for example, the winter solstice is the apex of the dark energy initiated at Samhain, and the summer solstice represents a mature expression of the bright summer energy kindled at Bealtaine. The energy of new life that begins at Imbolc reaches its peak at the spring equinox, while the harvest energy awakened at Lugnasadh reaches completion at the autumn equinox.

The journey through the Celtic year begins, as do all life journeys, in the darkness—in November when the land is dormant. Nothing appears to be happening, no outer activity. Yet deep within the earth, seeds are germinating and gathering energy for the journey ahead. Samhain, on November 1, is the first festival of the Celtic year and the gateway into the dark half of the year. During this season, which extends from November until February, darkness is the dominant experience for those living in the Celtic countries. In the northern hemisphere, the days get shorter, and darkness and night-time increase until the moment of the winter solstice around December 21, when darkness rules supremely.

After this moment of overwhelming darkness, the light begins to return gradually as the year moves towards the festival of Imbolc at the beginning of February. By this time, the rebirth of the sun seems secure. The sunlight continues to grow as the year moves towards the spring equinox, around March 21, when night and day, light and darkness are equal.

The increasing light continues to grow as the year flows towards Bealtaine on May 1. Bealtaine is the gateway into the bright half of the year. Light now becomes the dominant feature and increases in strength until the moment of the summer solstice, June 21, when the light is completely triumphant.

But this triumph of light is only momentary, because the gradual decline of the light also begins. The return journey is readily apparent as the year arrives at Lughnasadh on August 1, and the light continues to diminish through the autumn equinox around September 21, when day and night are again equal, and finally to the darkness of Samhain and the beginning of a new turn of the wheel of the year.

In this calendar, which measures time in seasons, each season holds a different quality of energy and has different tasks to accomplish. One season is not considered better than another. Each season flows from the one that preceded it and into the following one, creating a river of energy and life. Connections exist, too, between the festivals at opposite points on the wheel of the year, suggesting balance and symmetry. Samhain and Bealtaine both focus on the changes, independent of any human activity, that occur within the land itself. Imbolc and Lughnasadh both reflect the changing relationship between a people or society and their land.

Each of the eight annual festivals marks a particular conjunction of time and space. Each embodies a special moment in the year when the forces of nature are strongest in a particular direction. Living in close relationship with the seasons and the flowing of time allows us to be attuned to the earth and teaches us to co-operate with the energies of the season rather than fighting against them. The wheel of the year, when explored in all its dimensions, creates a greater context in which to place the reality of our lives.

When we view the Celtic year as a reflection of the agricultural year, which has both its beginning and ending at the time of darkness, it becomes possible to see that both sides of life's essential polarities are necessary as they flow into and out of each other in a natural and effortless way. Neither light nor darkness, day or night, life or death is better than the other in terms of energy. A time of darkness, of lying fallow, is as necessary as a time of brightness, of reaching for the sky. The dying of the grain at harvest time is as necessary as the first shoots of spring.

The dance of opposites

The Celtic mind has always been fascinated by the tension that exists in the polarities that underpin the reality of life. The seasons and festivals of the Celtic year themselves arise from the dialogue between light and darkness, permanence and change, movement and stillness. The Celtic mindset sees these opposing forces not in terms of conflict, but rather as polarities that dance with each other and in doing so create many new entities. It is this dance between the forces of light and darkness, between masculine and feminine energy, and between summer and winter that creates the different seasons and energies within the Celtic year—and also creates the colourful tapestries of our individual lives.

Relationships between pairs of opposites, such as day and night, also carry symbolic meaning, within the Celtic world. This is reflected in a story from the *Book of Leinster*:

> After the Dagda had apportioned all the *síd* mounds of Ireland between the lords of the Tuatha Dé Danann, the Mac Óc came to him and asked for land. "I have no land for thee," said the Dagda, "I have completed the division." "Then let me be granted a day and a night in thy own dwelling." That was given to him. "Go now to thy following," said the Dagda, "since thou hast consumed thy (allotted) time." "It is clear," said the Mac Óc, "that night and day are the whole world and it is that which has been given to me." Thereupon, the Dagda went out and the Mac Óc remained in his *síd*.[1]

In a variation of this tale, the Mac Óc claims the *síd* "in perpetuity on the grounds that 'it is in days and nights that the world is spent.'"[2] Having pondered this story many times, I wonder if it refers to the dance of these opposite energies of darkness and light, night and day, that weave the total tapestries of our lives. When we try to stop that dance by denying the presence of any single aspect of the life energy, the vibrancy of life is diminished, and we move from living to surviving. This is so evident in our culture, which tries to banish the darkness, death, and pain from our lives and to gain control over all the circumstances in our lives. What results from this attempt is a forced survival that may be safe, but lacks vibrancy and authenticity.

Circles and spirals

Both the circle and the spiral are central symbols in the world of the Celtic and pre-Celtic people. A circle is a line whose beginning and ending points meet to complete the circle; it is a closed structure. A spiral, however, is a circle that is not closed but continues to grow and expand out from a fixed point. With each turn of the spiral, a point is reached that corresponds to a previous location but resides at a different level. It is as if the circle is the unit or core, which holds the essential pattern, whose repetition creates the spiral with each turn.

This corresponds with the journey through the Celtic year, where the pattern of the circle—that is, the order and sequence of the seasons—is fixed and unfolds into a spiral as it is repeated each year. While the cycle of the year is constant, every spring or autumn is essentially different and unique. If we observe the seasons carefully, we will note that each spring or summer, different trees, plants, and flowers bloom more or less proficiently, and each autumn the colours of the leaves are different. These variations depend on the unique combination of sunshine, heat, darkness, rain, and wind present in that year.

So too, in the personal journey of our lives, we experience many springs, many winters, summers, and autumns, each of them different, each reflecting the unique interaction of the collection of circumstances in our lives at any particular moment in time. The same cycle is repeated, yet the outcome is slightly different each time. The cycle of growth and decay always follows the same basic pattern, but results in different manifestations with each turn of the spiral. Tuning into the different energies present within each season, we see them dance with each other, offer themselves completely to the world, fully present in each moment and yet constantly changing and evolving. This pattern offers us a blueprint for living, encouraging us to be at ease with change and flow. It helps us to understand that everything is part of a larger reality, and that everything comes from something and, in time, becomes something else. We begin to understand that there is only life, whose energy is expressed in its many different forms.

The Celtic Christian year

When Christianity came to Ireland, it took root in a way that reflected the essence of the spiritual and cultural mindset already present in Ireland at that time. This integration of the perennial Druidic wisdom into the Christian story is reflected in the unique expression of Christianity that unfolded and blossomed in Ireland until around the 10th century CE. At the time of the arrival of Christianity in Ireland, the ritual calendar of the Celtic year was deeply established within the psyche of the people. Rather than trying to dismiss this calendar, the Christian religion used it as a prototype on which to build the Christian liturgical year. Examining these calendars, we see many correspondences exist between the two. The integration of the pre-Christian Celtic festivals into the Christian liturgical year has ensured that much of the knowledge and practices of these earlier times has been kept alive within the Christian context. Making the journey around the Christian liturgical year allows us to explore some of these correspondences.

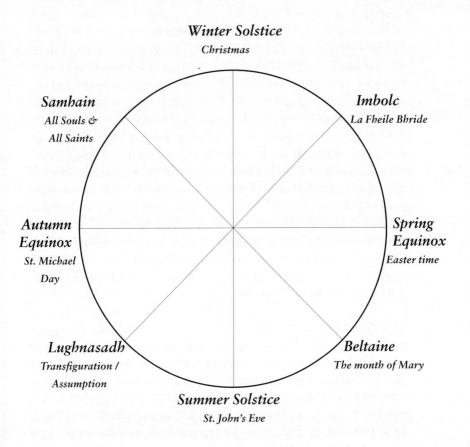

Figure 2
Celtic Christian Year

The festival of Samhain, as previously discussed, is the most significant festival in the Celtic year, a time when the veil between the worlds is thin and the gates that normally divide these worlds are open. The corresponding festivals in the Christian year are the feasts of All Saints and All Souls, where the attention of the church and the people is focused on the realm of the otherworld. On All Saints Day, November 1, the spotlight is on the communion of saints, while on All Souls Day, November 2, it is with the ancestors. At this time, prayers of intercession are made on behalf of those who have gone before us. These festivals have allowed people to connect with the communion of saints and with "all the worlds seen and unseen" as in ancient times.

The festival of Christmas, which celebrates the birth of the Divine Child, the Christ child who will become the saviour of humanity, strongly mirrors the celebration of the winter solstice. In both festivals, that which is born at this time—the new light and the divine child—must be hidden and protected until they are strong enough to emerge fully into the world of form.

Lá Fhéile Bríde, St. Brigid's feast day on February 1, and the Christian festival of Candlemas on the following day correspond with the Celtic festival of Imbolc. The lighting of candles to celebrate the returning light and encourage its growth was widespread all over Europe in pre-Christian times. Imbolc was associated with the emergence of new life and fertility embodied in the goddess Brigid. Many of the celebrations associated with this festival have been preserved in the rituals associated with Brigid in her Christian saint incarnation. There is a wealth of knowledge and practices associated with this festival that are still in use today. These are folk customs practised mostly in homes and at holy wells, rather than in churches.

Easter, the central festival in the Christian year, is a celebration of the resurrection of the crucified Christ and the new life that will ensue for humans. Here again, there is a correspondence with the spring equinox, also known as the festival of promise, which celebrates the returning new life after the death and bondage of winter. Since Easter in the Celtic Christian church was celebrated at a later date than in the Roman rite, there are also connections between Easter and Bealtaine. One custom that connects Easter and Bealtaine is that of going up to a high place on Easter morning or Bealtaine morning to see the sun dance. At Easter the sun is said to dance in praise of the risen Lord as is beautifully described in the following story collected by Alexander Carmichael:

> The people say that the sun dances on this day in joy for a risen Saviour. Old Barbara Macphie at Dreimsdale saw this once, but only once, during her long life. And the good woman, of high natural intelligence, described in poetic language and with religious fervour what she saw or believed she saw from the summit of Benmore:
>
> "The glorious gold-bright sun was after rising on the crest of the great hills, and it was changing colour—green, purple, red, blood-red, white, intense white, and gold-white, like the glory of the God of the elements to the children of men. It was dancing up and down in exultation at the joyous resurrection of the beloved Saviour of victory.
>
> "To be thus privileged, a person must ascend to the top of the highest hill before sunrise, and believe that the God who makes the small blade of grass to grow is the same God who makes the large, massive sun to move."[3]

Bealtaine, the summer season associated with fertility, blossoming, and flowers is mirrored in the Christian year with celebrations associated with both Mary, mother of Jesus, and with the Holy Spirit. In Ireland, even as late as the 1960s, processions in honour of Our Lady, Queen of the Angels and Queen of the May (Maybush) were commonplace. The connection of heaven to earth was proclaimed in the folk hymn, "Oh Mary, we crown thee with blossoms today, Queen of the Angels and Queen of the May." Many people created altars in their homes, filled with flowers, in honour of Our Lady. The Christian feast of Pentecost, in May or June, celebrates the coming of the Holy Spirit, who awakens new life in the human soul.

The correspondences in the summer half of the year are not as striking as those in the winter half, when most of the major Christian festivals occur. The Celtic Christians were followers of St. John, and this may explain the importance of his feast on June 24. This date, of course, corresponds with the summer solstice of the pre-Christian Celts. Bonfires are still lit in many places on St. John's Eve, even though the people lighting the bonfires may no longer know the reason or significance of the ritual.

The festival of Lughnasadh, which initiates the time of harvest, has a connection with two feasts of the Christian year. The Transfiguration of Christ, celebrated on August 6, expresses the first fruits of redemption. The rest of the faithful will follow with the Blessed Virgin Mary leading the way into heaven on the feast of her Assumption into heaven on August 15.[4] This in some way relates to the harvest of the soul during our life's journey.

The autumn equinox, with the completion of the harvest, is celebrated in Christian churches with Thanksgiving ceremonies held at or near that time. St. Michael, whose feast day is September 29, is often understood as the psychopomp, the one who goes before us into the underworld. His feast occurs at the time of preparation for the release of the year, which leads to the subsequent descent into the darker times.

These processions and celebrations associated with the different aspects of the agricultural year have now disappeared in many places, and I believe that we humans are the poorer for this. Seán Ó Duinn reflects how this disappearance has "left technological man with his technology, but with no liturgical reminder of his connection with the land or the cycle of the year."[5] Forgetting this inheritance has cost us a healthy counterweight to the linear concept of time predominant in industrial society, but we can restore it with renewed attention to the Celtic year.

The tyranny of endless day

It is neither possible nor desirable for people living in one era to try to live the lifestyle of another time. What is both possible and desirable, however, is that much valuable knowledge from previous times can be recovered and used in appropriate ways in our lives today. The cosmology of the people who created the Celtic year calendar and the rituals that celebrate the different festivals is such a rich source of essential wisdom. To understand how the Celtic year calendar and its underlying cosmology might be relevant to our present society, it is necessary to understand the mindset of the people who created it and compare this with the values and norms that underpin the society today. In this way, that which is important and valued and that which is not can be revealed. Reviewing this means asking how we, as a society, arrived at this present place: What choices were made, and what was lost as society moved forward? What remains?

As human beings living in the 21st century, our experience of the world is both larger and smaller than in previous times. While we have a greater capacity to access vast amounts of information instantly, travel faster, and consume vast amounts of material goods, we have a diminished sense of our own true nature and the nature of the universe. Ironically, it would seem that we lack a sense of our place and our role in the cosmos, even though we live primarily in the material world, ignoring the presence and influence of the non-physical and spiritual worlds. The world is understood and mostly experienced from the rational, logical perspective, with little value placed on the softer knowing of the intuition or imagination. Those worlds of soft colours and edges that might be experienced in candlelight, those worlds of subtle energies are at best marginalised and often banished. The world inhabited by the 21st century person is one of endless light, where there is, it seems, no desire for the darkness that might bring balance, diversity, and creativity into the world. It is a world of endless doing with no place for being, a world of endless growth with no place for integration, and a world with no time or place for rest and regeneration. This is a world of constant movement and striving, with little sense of belonging or communion. It is a restless world where there is little sense of home.

Today's world has arisen from the choices made over the previous few hundred years, during which great advances in scientific thought and in material progress have occurred. Since the time of the Enlightenment, people have attempted to transcend the limitations placed on them by the natural world, in particular the limitations associated with darkness and the lack of light. The introduction of electric light allowed us, as a society, to move past these limitations of darkness, night, and winter and offered to us the possibility of endless light. While these advances had many positive benefits, they also created problems. Once the possibility to enjoy endless light was valued by society, it proved difficult to choose to turn it off. Today's world values only the light and everything associated with light. Darkness is not a treasured asset. The nuances of life that might emerge from inhabiting the darkness are absent in the present society, and their gifts lost to us. As a result, the balance that would ensure a healthy lifestyle is missing, and this now dominant aspect of life has become dangerous and demonic. The world of western society insists on constant growth, endless doing, and endless summertime. Comparing how life is experienced within the present society with the pattern held within the calendar of the Celtic year, it is obvious that both a sense of balance and an understanding of the spiral of birth, life, death, and regeneration are missing today.

Reflection: Seed thoughts for the eight festivals

These questions, each of which relates to a festival and its season, may serve as seed thoughts for reflection or meditation at different times in the year or at different stages within your life journey.

Samhain

What do I need to let go of in my life? What needs to die at this moment?

Winter solstice
How can I become the seed of my own rebirth? What aspects of my life need regeneration?

Imbolc
What stirrings of new life are making themselves known to me?

Spring equinox
To what aspects of this new life within am I willing to commit myself?

Bealtaine
What aspects of self, talents, gifts, or projects am I willing to bring into the world of form at this time?

Summer solstice
What seeds sown at the winter solstice have now blossomed and ripened in my life?

Lughnasadh
What am I harvesting at this time? What skills have I perfected?

Autumn equinox
What is it that is now complete in my life?

Meditation: The year in review

Try doing this exercise at the time of year that most strongly means new beginnings to you. That could be Samhain, the last few days of December, or your birthday. For teachers, it might be the start of the new school year.

Take a few moments to centre yourself. Breathe out as deeply as you can, then breathe in as deeply as you can. Become aware of the ebb and flow of your breath for a few moments until you feel centred within yourself.

Take a few moments to review the past year of your life. As you reflect on the life journey you made, remember some of the events that happened. Notice how you experienced yourself at different times and in different circumstances during the past year.

Be aware of the different activities that happened during that space of time—the births, the deaths, the letting go, the nurturing, the blossoming, and the empty spaces. As you remember this past year, see if you can identify

- Moments of death and letting go
- Moments of waiting and emptiness
- Moments of new birth and new beginnings
- Moments of growth and strengthening
- Moments of flowering
- Moments of harvesting
- Moments of completion
- Moments of resting

Allow yourself to become aware of the diversity of experiences present within your life and give thanks for this year of your life, with all its many seasons and activities.

Reflection: Accepting the seasons

Bearing in mind the eight seasons of the Celtic year and the energies associated with them, ask yourself which seasons you find easiest to inhabit. Which ones are most difficult for you? What makes the energy of a certain season easy or difficult for you? How do you engage with these energies? How do you integrate them?

Once you have reviewed your present attitudes toward the seasons, look beyond: What would enable you to align yourself with the energies present in each season of the year instead of struggling against them? Is it possible for you to accept that all the seasons and energies are needed to create the tapestry of your life? Create a prayer or invocation that will help you welcome each season, with its unique energy, into your life.

The dance of light in darkness

The Celtic calendar emerges from a dance between the light and the darkness, as they mingle together to create a variety of experiences and seasons within the period of each year. The Celtic tradition is not alone in exploring the themes of light and darkness. For example, the soul's growth in the darkness, the penetration of the darkness by the light, and the resultant trans-formation of the darkness are concepts found in many cultures. It is interesting to observe that darkness is, in fact, an absence of light and needs only the presence of light for its transformation. Both darkness and light are essential in the soul journey.

Because the calendar and its rituals occupied a significant role in the spiritual life of the peoples of the Celtic lands, they retain, in symbolic form, many essential aspects of ancient spir-itual tradition. However, reconnecting with the Celtic tradition requires much more than just noting or even celebrating the different times of the year. It is about remembering another way of life and seeing life through a *súil eile* (another eye), one that supports a different worldview. What is needed is to recover a worldview that understands how human beings are embedded in the natural world and inextricably linked to the life and ac-tivity of all the realms within the universe.

It may be that the Celtic calendar, that essential gift from the Celtic tradition, will help us homeless and rootless western peo-ple to remember the truth of who we are and the relationships that underpin our reality. As we become familiar with the core of this tradition, it will be possible to adapt its themes to enrich our own lives, both by using elements from the Celtic seasonal rituals and by devising our own responses to the turn of the wheel of the year.

Chapter 8:

CELEBRATING THE CELTIC SEASONS

Since the spiritual and human life journeys for the Celtic and pre-Celtic peoples were completely interconnected, it was natural for their spiritual rituals to coincide with the observable agricultural and solar rhythms of the year. The resulting Celtic calendar can be seen as a wheel having eight stations—a mandala— with each station representing a coming together of cosmic forces in a certain direction at a certain time. These stations are located approximately 45 days apart. Each season with its special energy is a necessary component occupying a unique role in the mandala that represents the journey through the year. The festival and rituals associated with each station offer an opportunity for people to step outside of the mundane, day-to-day life and to connect with and honour the essence of the specific time and the energy associated with the season.

In past times, the annual repetition of these festivals each year created a sense of familiarity and security that offered people confidence, no matter at what stage of the life journey they found themselves. Small, simple family and community rituals at the turn of the seasons ensured that the quality or dimension of eternity was touched at regular intervals. Michael Dames, in *Mythic Ireland*, reflects on the role these rituals held in earlier times: "By house rites, the quality of eternity was touched at regular intervals and formalized into a reliable framework. A collective inner tranquillity thus survived the impact of physical hardship and remorseless change."[1]

The renewal of these rituals has the potential to awaken again this sense of connection and belonging within the lives of people and their communities. To more fully understand the festivals and their associated rituals, let us revisit these eight seasons that mark the cardinal points on the wheel or mandala representing the full year and explore the themes and practices associated with each one.

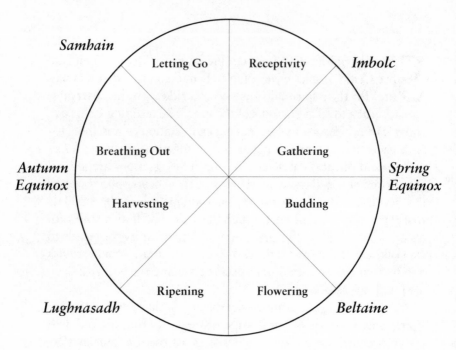

Figure 3
The Energies of the Celtic Year

Samhain

Let us begin this exploration at Samhain, the most significant festival in the Celtic calendar. This festival is celebrated at
a time considered to be "time out of ordinary time." Samhain
marks the beginning of the *giamos* season, the time of darkness, the realm of the goddess, where the feminine energy principle is experienced and the season of non-doing is initiated.[2] It
underpins the essence of the cosmology of this spiritual tradition as it holds the energies of beginnings and endings and the
relationship between them. Samhain celebrates the mysteries of
life, death, and rebirth present at the heart of Celtic spiritual
tradition.

One of the etymologies of the word Samhain suggests that
it means "three days at the end of summer." The actual Samhain festival consists of three nights and three days that belong
neither to the old year just completed nor to the new year that
has yet to begin. This festival marks the end of the agricultural
year: All the agricultural work must be completed, and whatever is not done by Samhain must be abandoned. This festival was
celebrated both at the Hill of Tara and a place called Tlachtga
near Athboy in County Meath, where the fire of the new year
was lit and brought to Tara for use in the rituals.

The principal themes associated with the festival of Samhain are:

Opening of the gates between the worlds
The veil between this world and the otherworld is thin, making it easier for us to connect with other dimensions and the
beings who reside there.

Hospitality for the dead, our ancestors
At Samhain, it is customary to connect with, pray for, and
appeal to our ancestors, those people who have journeyed
before us on this earth. In so doing, we can perhaps claim
their gifts and be involved in the healing of their wounded-
ness. This age-old custom is still honoured today within the
Christian tradition as the feasts of All Saints (November 1)
and All Souls (November 2).

Loosening of normal societal behaviours
Celtic society was very structured, with each person and group having their assigned place and role. During Samhain, the normal rules of society were relaxed, allowing people to step outside their normal conventions. People dressed in strange clothes and played tricks on their neighbours and superiors. While order was important within the tribe, it was also understood that its occasional absence was necessary to restore balance. The energy of chaos was invited into the tribe and society in a controlled way, perhaps to shake things up and so move society to a new balance point, just as the old year is released to make room for the new year. Here we experience an essential aspect of the Celtic cosmology—the ever present dance of polarities that creates the dynamic experience of life.

Timelessness
Since this was "time out of time," it was customary to engage in divination, and many different types of fortune telling were practised. This is the origin of many traditional games played during Hallow E'en in Ireland (or Halloween, as it is known in some countries) until recent times.

Sacrifice
Offerings were made to the earth and the spirits that resided in it, in thanksgiving for the harvest. Some of the fruits harvested in the current cycle were given in total sacrifice to the earth, so that a new cycle might begin. The seeds entered into the darkness of the earth in order to bring forth a new and more abundant life when the winter period of darkness and apparent death are over. Any animal that was considered too weak to survive throughout the winter was slaughtered, the blood poured into the earth as an offering to the land and the flesh cured for consumption during the winter months.

Renewal
This was the time when both the earth and humans prepared to rest. As the days darkened after Samhain, there was very little outward activity, and so the energy was gathered inwards to support what was happening deep within the earth and deep within the human psyche. The energy gathered in this season would be used later when winter had passed and spring brought new life to both the land and the people.

Release
Whatever is not completed at this time must be released, because the year with its set of seasons is now over. Any unfinished agricultural work must be abandoned. The light must be released, also the *samos* energy of activity and doing. What is required in this season is for humans to surrender into the *giamos* mode of being, into the darkness, active waiting, and non-doing that characterises this time.

Samhain marks the beginning of the winter season, when traditionally most activity was home-centred and inwardly focused, much of the outer activity having ceased. As the days grew shorter, the nights got longer, and darkness and death were constant companions. Death was present all around now, in the fallow fields, in the bare trees, and in the sleeping earth. Presiding over the season is the *cailleach* or hag aspect of the Goddess or the divine feminine, which is connected with death and decay, but ultimately leads to rebirth and new life. The only activity possible is that which occurs deep within the earth. The natural response of a person living in harmony with this season would be to draw one's energy inward and limit the outer activity, in harmony with the *giamos* time associated with the principle of renewal within the womb of the earth.

Winter solstice

The winter season extends from November until February. From Samhain until the winter solstice—when the longest night of the year occurs, around December 21—the light is decreasing, and the life-force energy is being drawn deeper into the earth. The dominant movement is that of sinking and surrendering to the inevitable void and abyss that is the darkness of mid-December in the northern hemisphere. This time of winter solstice—the word *solstice* means "sun stands still"—represents the experience of ultimate darkness and emptiness and yet is, paradoxically, a time of great fecundity. The still darkness yields to a point of turning and to the beginning of the second part of the winter season, when the slow journey from that place deep within the earth begins to move in an outward direction towards spring and new life.

The journey from Samhain to the winter solstice is a path of continual sinking and letting go, of deep surrender. The days shorten; the nights get longer; the earth draws its energy deep within; death and darkness surround us. We reside in the womb or cauldron of the Goddess where gestation and transformation happen. We are deep within the *giamos* period, where the experience of linear time is minimised, willpower is muted, and contemplation of the ever-present form or ground of being, from which everything arises, is encouraged.[3] Here the mode of being that is required is rest, passive attentiveness to the unconscious influences of the otherworld, together with openness to growth that is slow and unforced. This is the dream time, where the seeds of new life, new ideas, and new projects are nurtured.

The principal themes present in the Celtic celebrations of the winter solstice are:

Acceptance and surrender
We must surrender to the ubiquitous darkness and inhabit the emptiness and the void. We must confront our fear of death and darkness.

Community support

Since the darkness is a difficult place for most people, we acknowledge the importance of family and community support for each other's journey through the darkness. Attending social gatherings and exchanging presents strengthen those shared links.

The birth of the new light in the midst of the darkness

At the winter solstice, the seed of light is born in the womb of the dark night of the year. This theme is wonderfully expressed in the ritual that has happened on every winter solstice morning at Newgrange (Uaimh Na Gréine) for at least the past 5,000 years. At dawn on the days of the winter solstice, people gather both inside and outside the monument to greet the rising sun. Those inside the mound wait in complete darkness for the thin ray of light to travel up along the passage and finally enter the large chamber at the centre of the monument. The tiny ray of light illuminates the whole chamber and the carvings on the various stones present in the recesses of the central chamber. This is a truly awesome experience. The ritual celebrates the new child of light born in the midst of darkness.

Nurture of the new light

Because of the fragile nature of the new light, it is necessary to nurture and protect that light until it is strong enough to manifest in the outer world. Likewise, the Divine Child, born at this time, must be hidden until it is strong enough to be present in the outer world. Within the Druidic tradition, the mistletoe is the symbol for the new Divine Child. This is the reason it is used in the ritual celebrations at this time of year.

When the winter solstice has passed, the journey back out from the depth of darkness and winter begins, making its way towards spring.

Imbolc

Imbolc, on February 1, divides the *giamos* half of the year into winter and spring. The season of Imbolc marks the very first signs of springtime and new life. An older version of this name is Imbolg, which means "in the belly," and gives rise to a beautiful metaphor that describes this time as "winter pregnant with summer." The seeds of summer are still hidden deep in the earth, in the womb of the Goddess, and, while the worst of the darkness of winter is over, spring has not yet fully arrived. It is, however, a time of hope and possibility.

This season is also known as Oimelc, a word connected with the first flowing of milk in the udders of the ewes, a month or so before the lambing season. This flow of milk is seen as a harbinger of the awakening of the land, together with the return of fertility to the earth, as true springtime unfolds. The essence of this season is the welcoming of the returning light and a celebration of the stirring of the life force, or *neart*, in the land.

Imbolc is synonymous with Brigid, Celtic goddess and saint, who embodies the energy of new life and of new beginnings. She is the fertile aspect of the divine feminine energy, which emerges from the hag or *cailleach*, the dark, barren aspect of the feminine energy. This transformation of the *cailleach* into the maiden reflects the same mysteries that are occurring in the natural world as winter yields to spring.[4] Brigid is the energy that breathes life into the mouth of dead winter. She is the fertility goddess who embodies the *neart* or life force, that raw primal feminine energy that gives rise to all living beings. The name Brigid has many meanings associated with it. One such meaning from the root word, *briga*, is hills and mountains, implying that Brigantia might mean "she who raises herself on high, who is exalted." According to Alexi Kondratiev, it suggests in some Celtic languages "force, power, meaning, invigorating essence."[5] The festival of Imbolc celebrates the re-awakening of fertility in the land and the inception of a new cycle of agricultural activity, with Brigid, the creative force, present in both the people and the land, uniting them together. The fire of Brigid was both the fire of fertility within the earth and the fire of the sun, now growing in strength each day. The elements of fire and water, which both play an essential role in the fertility of the land, are associated with Brigid and her festivals.

The main themes associated with the festival of Imbolc are:

Re-Awakening the life force

In a celebration held in people's homes, Brigid crosses were woven from rushes, blessed, and distributed for use in the coming year. A doll or *babóg* representing Brigid was also made from straw or rushes. The youngest member of the family, holding the *babóg* would knock on the door and ask, "*An Bhfúil Fáilte sa teach seo roimh Brigid?*" (Is there a welcome in this house for Brigid?)

To which those inside the house replied, "*Tar isteach! Ta fáilte romhat! Se Beatha Se Beatha Se Beatha A Bhrid Naofa.*" (Come inside! You are welcome! She is life, She is life, She is life, Blessed Brigid.)

Celebrating the returning light

Candles were lighted in profusion to celebrate the more abundant light already visible and to press the sun to keep shining and grow in strength.[6] This Imbolc blessing encourages and celebrates the growing light: "May the light of inspiration grow in our hearts and between us as the year unfolds and the light increases."

Purification with water

At Imbolc, the hands, feet, and head were washed to consecrate them for the new cycle of work and to remove any remaining *giamos* energy that might impede growth in this new cycle.[7] Visiting a Holy well dedicated to Brigid was another very common ritual practice at this festival. Water would be taken from the well and used for healing throughout the year.

Brat Bhride

It was customary to hang a cloth on a bush, usually a haw-thorn bush, on the eve of this festival so that when Brigid passed through the land that night, she would touch the cloth and impart healing energies to it. This cloth then would be used for healing during the year.

After Imbolc, signs of spring continue to emerge, and the year moves towards the time of equal day and night in the northern hemisphere.

Spring equinox

As the life force continues to grow in strength, the sun be-comes stronger, the daylight increasing until the spring (vernal) equinox is reached around March 21, when day and night are equal in length in the northern hemisphere. True spring has ar-rived, and there is reason to believe that the seeds sown deep in winter will blossom and create the crops that will unfold in the fullness of time

The spring equinox, also known as the festival of promise, is a further celebration of the return of spring and the grow-ing light. The sun continues to grow in strength, changing the ratio of darkness to light. Those seeds hidden and nurtured deep within the earth in the dark time are now getting ready to emerge.

An important custom for this festival was to go to a high place to greet the rising sun and welcome the growing spring-time. At Sliabh na Cailli (Lough Crew) in County Meath, the rising sun shines into a cairn and lights the decorated stone at the back of the chamber of Cairn T, one of many cairns in that ancient complex. To be present at Lough Crew at this time is a truly wonderful experience.

As the sun continues its journey of increase, the year moves inevitably towards Bealtaine, summer, and the *samos* mode of being.

Bealtaine

Continuing the journey around the wheel of the year, we arrive at the festival of Bealtaine, which stands diametrically opposite to Samhain and is the second most important festival in the Celtic calendar. While Samhain time is associated with the ancestors and the world of spirits, Bealtaine is connected with the material world and its fertility. As Samhain is associated with the Goddess and feminine energy, Bealtaine is associated with the God and masculine energy. The festival of Bealtaine marks the final transition point from a season dominated by inward activity to one of outward activity. It marks the crossing over from the *giamos* to the *samos* mode of being, when action is encouraged, linear causality in time dominates, and things happen in an explicate and rapid fashion. This is the gate into the bright half of the year, which marks the beginning of the summer, and is another time when the veils between the worlds are thin. The countryside is filled with the white blossoms of the hawthorn and the translucent greenness of the new foliage. It is the season associated with the Flower Maiden and with the god Belenos, the bright one, who is associated with the healing powers of the sun. This season initiates outdoor activities and the celebration of summer.

The following themes are reflected in the celebration of Bealtaine:

Purification with fire

In times past, cattle that had been indoors all winter were walked through the fire at Bealtaine to purify them before they went out to summer pastures. This ritual can be modified and used by today's celebrants, who can use the fires of Bealtaine to purify any leftover winter negativity that might impede the *samos* activity and growth in their lives or projects.

The Flower Maiden

The Flower Maiden represents the fertile aspect of the land goddess, the young mother. She is celebrated at this time and honoured especially with flowers, which are strewn on the doorsteps and roofs of houses, beckoning the fertility she represents into all aspects of one's life. In former times, altars were created in homes and schools in honour of the returning fecundity of the land, and the Flower Maiden was celebrated in processions by young girls singing and carrying armloads of flowers through towns and villages.

Sacred marriage of masculine and feminine energies
The masculine energy of activity emerges from the passive state it occupied during the *giamos* period and becomes the dominant energy in this *samos* time. This is represented by the young god of summer, Maponos, who woos the Flower Maiden, wins her from the winter king, and marries her. Maypole rituals celebrate this marriage of the masculine and feminine energies. This masculine energy acts in the service of the seeds sown and nurtured by the feminine energy during winter and spring, the *giamos* season. In the Celtic tradition, the masculine and feminine energies are represented by fire and water and are considered to be most effective when they act together in harmony with each other. On May morning, it was customary for people to go to the top of a hill before sunrise, light fires in honour of the sun, and bathe in the rays of the sun as it rose on the first day of summer. They washed their faces in the early morning dew, which was considered a magical substance as it consisted of fire and water, capable of ensuring youth and vitality. Others went to holy wells and drank the water or poured water over themselves as at the rays of the rising sun hit the water.[8] All of these customs and rituals reflect this power of water and fire working together and the potency of masculine and feminine energy working in harmony within the land, a person, or a project.

Summer solstice

The journey of increasing light continues with the approach of mid-summer, around June 21 in the northern hemisphere, when the light triumphs and brightness occupies a large part of both day-time and night-time hours. High summer celebrates the complete blossoming and fruition of the seeds sown back in the depths of winter. However, this triumph of light is, like all things, transitory. Just as the journey toward the summer solstice began at the time of the winter solstice, so too the journey back to the winter solstice is initiated at this moment. The sun begins to lose some of its strength; it shines for a shorter time each day, as the year moves past the summer solstice. The water energy, in the form of rain—so much a part of summer in the northern regions—tempers the fire energy and ensures that the crops reach full ripeness without being burned.

Key themes for the summer solstice are:

Storing the light

At midsummer, the focus is on preserving and storing as much of the nourishing light as possible. The element of fire, which represents the sun's fertilising power, was ritually brought into contact with the land and crops to ensure good growth. People also jumped over the fire to gain a blessing from this powerful element, taking the fire energy into themselves and storing it to be used as a protection in later times of darkness or uncertainty.[9]

Harvesting of herbs

Much of the sun's energy was stored in plants that had been actively growing since spring, and so the harvesting of herbs to be used in the coming year was an important task associated with the summer solstice festival. The herbs harvested at this time included St. John's wort (*Hypericum perforatum*), Yarrow (*Achillea millefolium*), and Meadowsweet (*Filipendula ulmaria*).[10]

Lughnasadh

Lughnasadh, on August 1, divides the *samos* season into summer and autumn. It begins the harvest season, which represents the successful outcome of the working relationship between the people and their land that had begun the previous Samhain. As the crops were harvested, the people gathered to celebrate this success, which was crucial to the survival of the community.

Lughnasadh stands diametrically opposite to Imbolc, where Brigid, embodying the primal creative energy, occupied the central role. Lughnasadh honours the god Lugh, the *samildanach* or many-gifted one, who represents the skilled masculine energy with its ability to hone, shape, and bring to harvest the fruits of the seeds planted at Samhain and nurtured during the *giamos* time by the feminine energy. Here again, the important dance of opposite energies and roles is beautifully expressed in multiple ways. Tailtiu, the foster mother of Lugh, is the goddess who cleared away the wilderness, making the plains and fields ready for crops to be grown. She died from her efforts and is also remembered at this time; Lugh is said to have inaugurated the festival in her honour.

Bron Trogain, an older name for this festival, may mean the sorrow of Trogain or the sorrow of the fertile earth. This may indicate that the fertility of the harvest is linked with the death that follows its completion, again bringing together the polarities of life and death. The successful harvest requires that Lugh appease his adversary, Crom Dubh, who represents the aspect of the land that does not wish to be harvested or subjected to the rule and energy of Lugh. The last Sunday in July occurs just before the festival of Lughnasadh and is known as Crum Dubh's Sunday.

The two-week Lughnasadh festival was a very important meeting time for the tribe, bringing people together to test their skills in many different disciplines. They challenged each other in a variety of contests and games held during the annual fairs or *aonachs* in Lugh's honour. The rituals at this festival included the acknowledgement of the triumph of Lugh, the harvesting and enjoyment of the first fruits, and the acknowledgment of the end of summer. It was a time of great merriment, especially for young people, who wore garlands of flowers and went into the hills to pick bilberries or blueberries. Marriages were traditionally held at this time of year.

High places in the land, where earth and sky met, were considered the appropriate place to honour Lugh. At the ritual site, many of the characteristics and gifts of Lugh were enacted by mummers. The first sheaf of wheat, barley, or corn was ceremonially cut, milled, and baked into cakes to be ceremonially eaten along with the wild blueberries or bilberries. The young folks' garlands of flowers were buried to signify the end of summer.

Many of these ritual practices associated with Lughnasadh have died out, but an essential aspect of the Lughnasadh ritual is enacted each year with the annual pilgrimage to Croagh Patrick in County Mayo on the last Sunday in July. Puck Fair held in Kilorglin in County Kerry each August is another remnant of the Lughnasadh festival.

Autumn equinox

As the year continues to turn, decreasing daylight and the loss in strength of the sun's energy point to the coming of the autumn equinox around September 21, where again day and night are equal. This time is associated with the completion of the harvest and is a time of thanksgiving for what has been accomplished in this cycle. It also is the beginning of the final descent toward the year's end at Samhain. This period between the autumn equinox and Samhain is understood as a "breathing out" time as the end of the cycle approaches.

As the harvesting activity reaches its peak, the themes celebrated around the equinox are a conclusion of those inaugurated at Lughnasadh—thanksgiving for the fruit of people's labours and the accomplishment of the full harvest. The preservation of the fertility of the land is maintained through the burial of the last sheaf of grain. This is a time of release, a time to prepare for the coming of the *giamos* time where action must be muted and the light must yield to the darkness.

Reflection: Inner and outer

Focus on your out-breath and in-breath for a few moments to allow yourself to become quiet inside. Let the ebb and flow of your breath bring you into a deep and quiet space.

In this quiet place, become aware of the Celtic year with its eight different seasons and festivals. Samhain, winter solstice, Imbolc, spring equinox, Bealtaine, summer solstice, Lughnasadh, and autumn equinox.

Reflect on the fallowness of Samhain, the darkness of the winter solstice, the almost imperceptible new growth of Imbolc, the gradual growing of light and activity at the spring equinox, the blossoming energy of Bealtaine, the fullness and ripeness of the summer solstice, the gathering energy of harvest at Lughnasadh, the energy of completion at the autumn equinox, and the breathing out as Samhain again approaches. Each season and its associated energies span a roughly six-week period during which the energy changes in subtle ways as the focus shifts from inner to outer or from outer to inner. Reflect on the energies associated with the different seasons, noticing which ones are outwardly focused and oriented toward activity and those that are inwardly focused and inclined toward receptivity.

Pick one of the seasons in the year. Focus on that season for a few moments. Be aware of the predominant energy and activity of that season. Now become aware of the season that comes before it and the season that comes after it. Be aware of the energies present in these seasons, and notice how the energy associated with these seasons flows in and out of each other— Imbolc flowing out of winter solstice and into spring equinox, Bealtaine flowing into summer solstice, Lughnasadh flowing out of summer solstice, Samhain flowing out from autumn equinox—creating a river of energies that change as each year unfolds in its own unique way.

Reflection: Embracing the seasons

Bring your awareness to the ebb and flow of your breath as you breathe in and out. Allow each breath to bring you into a deep quiet place inside yourself.

In this quiet place, take a few moments to reflect on your own life situation at this time, acknowledging the reality of your life rather than some idealised version of how it should be. Reflect for a moment on the eight seasons of the Celtic year and their energies, noting that some are focused outwards, others inwards. Some celebrate outer activity, while others celebrate waiting and inner reflection.

As you consider these energies and seasons, ask yourself how the various seasons reflect the different aspects of your life at this time. Consider your personal, family, spiritual, and work lives, and reflect on each separately. For each aspect of your life, ask yourself to which season or energy it is currently most attuned. As you identify the season or energy associated with each part of your life ask yourself what challenges this season presents to that aspect of your life. What would support you as you embrace this season? What skills do you need? What gifts can be harvested, for your soul journey, by being present in this season? How might being present in this season enable you to flow with grace into the next season of your journey?

Embracing the wheel of the year

One cycle has now been completed, and we arrive again at Samhain, ready to celebrate the three days and nights that separate the old and the new years and represent "time out of time." This pattern of life underpinned the calendar that organised the universe and reality for people living in the northern countries for many centuries. In celebrating the old festivals, we honour a sense of time that has been considered sacred for thousands of years. We align ourselves with the cosmic rhythm and create a sense of connection with a universe more expansive than our small private world. The celebration of the festivals acknowledges how humans are inextricably linked with the life and activities happening in all realms. This allows a person or community to be in contact with that eternal dimension of life and gives a confidence with which to meet the trials and joys of every day.

In the Celtic year, each of its eight distinct festivals has associated myths that reveal deep truths on both the personal and cosmological levels. The rituals for each of these festivals are the grounding actions of the myths connected with each particular season. These emerge from the cosmological and spiritual vision held by the society, each practice reflecting the mythology of the particular festival. As people living in the 21st century, with a different worldview and understanding of life, these practices and rituals may seem strange or superstitious to us. We may believe that they have no relevance in our lives. Yet the fundamental relationship that exists between humans and the natural world and that underpins this cosmology has not changed significantly in the past 2,000 years.

However, the stories and myths reflecting these earlier relationships between humans and the natural world have been replaced by new stories—stories that emphasise the dominance of the human being over the natural world. This new mythology, which alienates and separates humans from the natural world, is neither sustainable nor desirable and diminishes our humanity. I believe that recovering the wisdom present in Celtic tradition and its understanding of the seasons of the year will support the finding of a new and more sustainable story by which to order our lives.

Chapter 9:

THE RHYTHM OF LIFE
IS A POWERFUL BEAT!

D. H. Lawrence once said, "Mankind has got to get back to the rhythm of the cosmos."[1]Acknowledging the rhythm of life as it unfolds gives a dynamism and vibrancy to living and creates a sense of freshness and belonging. When in tune with this rhythm, one obtains a sense of being at home both within oneself and in the world. The many Celtic stories pertaining to time and to seasons suggest that the Celtic mind has always been fascinated by the tension between novelty and conformity, between order and chaos, between movement and stillness, and between light and darkness.[2] There was an understanding that the tension arising between these polarities was the very creative force that gave life its vitality and resulted in the creation of "the many thousand things." The Celtic mind saw the world as a place filled with diversity, where life was experienced as a rich tapestry woven from the interplay of opposite energies, constantly unfolding into being, and bringing forth both newness and surprise.

This aspect of the Celtic mind is beautifully reflected in a story from Fionn Mac Cumaill and the Fianna. Fionn and his warriors were discussing the various sounds in the world, each one telling what they considered to be the best sound. When Fionn was asked, "Which sound do you say is the best sound in the world?" he replied, "The music of what happens."[3] This story reminds us that life unfolds for each of us as an experience of the music of what happens and is—if we choose and allow it—the most beautiful sound in the world. In responding fully to life, we each add our unique sound to the unfolding symphony of the universe.

Life's journey . . . the Celtic pattern

Having discussed the actual Celtic year with its seasons, festivals, and rituals in Chapters 7 and 8, I now would like to focus on how the rhythm held within this calendar can act as a guiding principle for the human and spiritual journey. From the many possible correspondences between moments in our lives and the seasons of the Celtic year, I would like to explore how this pattern relates to:

- The overall journey of life
- The smaller cycles within the larger journey
- The spiritual and psychological journey
- The creative process
- The time scale of any professional or personal project

Philip Carr-Gomm has illustrated how the calendar mirrors the actual journey of life, from conception to old age and death, in a diagram, which I have adapted in Figure 4[4]:

This frame of reference allows people to locate their time on earth within a bigger context, seeing their lives as emerging from the season of Samhain and the otherworld dimension, returning to that other dimension again at Samhain, at their deaths. Thus, the circle of the year's turning can be understood as part of a greater spiral of life and belonging.

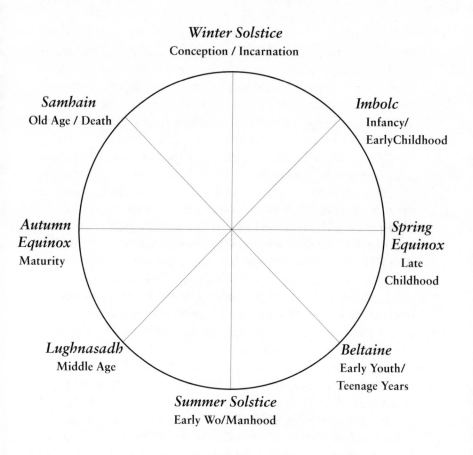

Figure 4
The Celtic Year and the human life cycle

The diagram in Figure 5 illustrates the constantly changing energies that are experienced during the eight seasons of the year. During the season of Samhain until the time of the winter solstice, the predominant energy is that of letting go and of death. This energy changes at the moment of the winter solstice to one of active waiting and receptivity, which presides until Imbolc. As the wheel of the year continues to move, there is again a shift in the type of energy experienced, a small movement from inward to outward focus as the spring equinox approaches. This outward trend strengthens as the year moves towards Bealtaine. As the season of Bealtaine unfolds into high summer, the energy continues its outward focus, reaching peak activity at the summer solstice. Now at its apex, the outward energy begins to move inwards with the harvesting and gathering activities of Lughnasadh and the autumn equinox, and a shift occurs towards the inner expression as Samhain approaches once again.

This pattern of alternating inward- and outward-moving energies is repeated many times during one's grand life journey— in creating a marriage, raising a family, entering a career, and taking on a project. All of these tasks and activities will have their own moments and seasons corresponding to those within the Celtic calendar cycle. Energies will ebb and flow, will reach high and low points, and will have times of quiet inward focus and times of vibrant outward direction within the lifetime of any project or relationship. When we understand how each of these seasons and their attendant energies flows into and out from the others, creating a river of experiences, we are sustained and supported as we embrace everything that life offers us.

At any one time, different aspects of our lives will be located in different seasons of the calendar, and each will elicit its own specific response. While there is a correlation between the seasons of the year and those of our lives, there also are times when our lives are out of sync with the external season. So, while seasonally it might be Samhain, we might be occupying a Bealtaine season within our own lives.

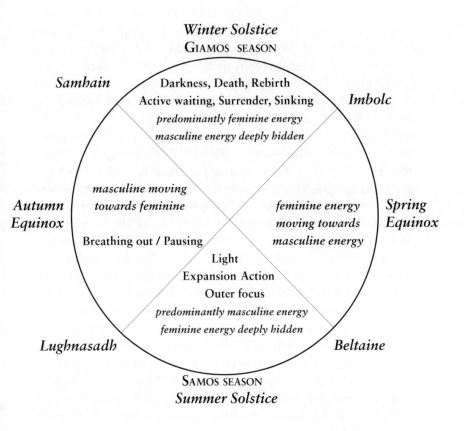

Figure 5
The Dance of masculine and feminine energies within the Celtic Year

Embracing the Samhain seasons of our lives

The seasonal flow within our own lives may also be suddenly disrupted. Everything may be blossoming when suddenly some crisis throws us headlong into the darkness of Samhain, with its chaotic energy. This can happen when we lose a job or lose a marriage through divorce or death, when serious illness strikes us or a loved one, or when any other event visits us unexpectedly. At such a time, understanding the energy of this Samhain season and the skills needed to negotiate its terrain can be very useful. This is especially true since the response to unwelcome change or death normally encouraged within western society is that of fight or flight. Embracing the actual reality of the moment and engaging with it in a deep way is discouraged. Fighting to maintain the status quo or moving as quickly as possible towards a new beginning is the preferred option. At the heart of this response is the fear of death, so predominant within the psyche of people in western society. This covers not only the fear of physical death, but also the fear of dying to outmoded ideas, to social norms, or to positions of power. This fear of death stifles the creative energy within us, encouraging plausible but mediocre responses to life, while denying the possibility of real transformation. Put in terms of the metaphor of the calendar, society encourages us to skip the dark season and its energy and move directly from November (Samhain) to February (Imbolc), avoiding the winter solstice at mid-December, that place of darkness and emptiness, which is also the place of deep fecundity, renewal and rebirth. This refusal to enter into the darkness and the abyss is at the root of all addictive and co-dependent behaviours. The inability to stop and embrace what life is offering in each moment encourages the myriad of distracting behaviours that create so much busyness in people's lives in today's world.

Kahlil Gibran speaks of the consequences of refusing to enter the abyss in *The Prophet*, "You will cry but not all of your tears, and you will laugh but not all of your laughter."[5] David Whyte, in his poem "The Well of Grief," reflects on the consequences when we refuse to enter these dark places of grief, loss, and pain:

Those who will not slip beneath
the still surface on
the well of grief
turning downwards through its black water
to the place we cannot breathe
will never know the source from which we drink
the secret water, cold and clear,
nor find in the darkness glimmering
the small round coins
thrown by those who wished for something else.[6]

Addicted as we are to life and light, one of the most ben-
eficial gifts that the Celtic calendar offers us, personally and
as a society, is an understanding of the Samhain season and
its importance in our lives. The central myth of regeneration,
which occurs through the sequence of birth, death, and rebirth,
assures us that all life begins in the dark womb of creation and
emerges into new life in the fullness of time. The Celtic calendar
teaches the essential role of death and darkness within the life
journey, together with an assurance that death and darkness
are, in fact, very safe places.

Furthermore, the calendar teaches that, when we enter a
Samhain time in any aspect of our lives or when our society as
a whole is passing through Samhain, the most appropriate response is to embrace the inevitable darkness and chaos present.
It teaches us that being (rather than doing), reflecting, letting
go, active waiting, and surrender—are the spiritual tools with
which to negotiate the terrain of this season. It encourages us to
surrender to that dark place, the void, and allow it to work its
deep healing on us.

This is, of course, extremely challenging for people who
strive to have all the answers and be in control. Yet for those
who recognise it, this teaching can provide an inspiration, as
in the example of King George VI, who in his Christmas Day
broadcast in 1939, quoted the poet Minnie Louise Haskins:

I said to the man who stood at the gate of the year: "Give me a light that I may tread safely into the unknown." And he replied: "Go out into the darkness and put your hand into the Hand of God. That shall be to you better than light and safer than a known way." So I went forth, and finding the Hand of God, trod gladly into the night. And he led me towards the hills and the breaking of day in the lone East.[7]

In mythology, the void is represented by the cauldron, which appears in many of the Celtic myths. In these stories, the raw, unpalatable things are transformed during cooking, though the action of fire and water, into nourishing food. Embracing this wisdom, we learn to surrender to the force of transformation. We also learn that death, while inevitable, is not final and that new life always emerges from the space vacated by that which died or was transformed. We can then move forward, empowered and reborn, into the next stage of our life journey. If we embrace this wisdom in response to the many Samhain times we encounter, we will still experience pain and loss, but engaging with this pain will lead to transformation, to soul growth, and ultimately to healing our fear of death.

The creative process

Just as the Celtic calendar is a useful companion for the seasons of our lives, so too can it be a guiding influence in the creative process as it unfolds, whether in the making of a piece of artwork or in any personal, professional, or communal project. The diagram in Figure 6 explores how the energies within the different seasons of the year correspond with the tasks required in the different stages in the creative process.

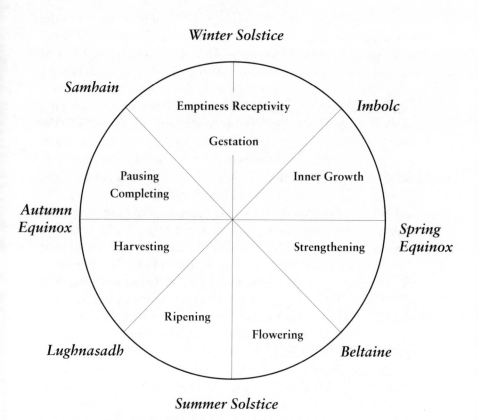

Winter Solstice

Samhain

Emptiness Receptivity

Imbolc

Gestation

Pausing
Completing

Inner Growth

*Autumn
Equinox*

Harvesting

Strengthening

*Spring
Equinox*

Ripening

Flowering

Lughnasadh

Beltaine

Summer Solstice

Diagram 6- The Creative Process

I believe that, in any creative project, the extent of ripening determines the quality of the end product and is, in turn, related to the amount of time and space allocated for reflection at the beginning of the process. In the language of the Celtic calendar, the fruits of the period between the summer solstice and Lughnasadh depend on the inner work done between Samhain and the winter solstice. Limiting the time spent in this early stage by prematurely skipping over to Imbolc results in a lack of connection with the seeds of the new project and with the creative energy hidden in the deep places within. The consequence of trying to bring up new, green shoots too soon is, paradoxically, to reduce creativity. What emerges into the world is a shrunken version of the initial dream or project.

If the artificial acceleration continues in such a scenario, the project will tend to move from Bealtaine to Lughnasadh, from first blossoming directly to harvest, and so avoid the full ripening at the summer solstice. This outcome reflects a lack of time spent in the reflective season of Samhain and an inability to reach the deep fertile place of the winter solstice. The result is mediocrity, which is a highly valued commodity in our society.

All creative processes require a balance of right-brained, intuitive and left-brained, analytical activities. Comparing the creative process with the seasons of the Celtic Year, we can correlate the intuitive, right-brained aspects with the inwardly reflective season of winter, the period from Samhain to Imbolc. In this season, the feminine energy of receptivity, the harnessing of new life force at the winter solstice, and the raw primal energy of creation at Imbolc dominate. As the creative process unfolds towards Bealtaine, the masculine energy becomes stronger and joins with the feminine energy until, at Bealtaine, it becomes the dominant force as the project or process moves out into the world of form so that it can be brought to harvest at Lughnasadh. In the harvest season, the masculine energy is needed to craft the final shape of the project. What this teaches us is that the successful outcome of any creative process requires a balancing dance of masculine and feminine energies, using each energy at the appropriate time in the process.

Welcome all four seasons

Using the Celtic year calendar as a model for our own lives, we learn that there is no Bealtaine without Samhain, no summer without winter, no blinding light without piercing darkness. Understanding this calendar, we learn how to live in ways that honour both halves of the year, the seasons of *giamos* and *samos*. By following the path of the year and understanding the energies associated with each season, we learn to perceive the complex and subtle energies present within ourselves and the universe. With this knowledge, we can come to inhabit these different energies and to cooperate with—rather than fight against—whatever is present in our lives in each moment. This brings more balance and harmony, greater creativity and productivity into our lives. When we can embrace the pattern of the year's turning in all aspects of our lives, as it moves from inner hidden activity to delicate budding to blossoming, flowering, ripening, harvesting, and breathing out, we are weaving the life energy as it flows though us, deepening and enriching our lives. Living life in this way provides a powerful counterbalance to the endless materialism and consumerism that contribute to our present graceless and soulless society. Learning to honour all of the energies within ourselves and the natural world will enable each of us to bring our inner and outer worlds together and live with integrity and vitality.

Understanding the basic premise of the Celtic calendar will enable us to relate to the rituals, practices, and beliefs held within it not from a place of superstition, but from an understanding of the cosmology and spirituality of the people who created it. Using the calendar as a blueprint we can ask, "How do we, in the midst of our modern lives, honour and celebrate this ancient spirit of time?"

Epilogue

"Now is the time and we are the ones that we have been waiting for."
—Hopi Indian statement, 2002

At the beginning of second decade of the 21st century, there is undeniable evidence that the way in which human beings now live is having a very serious impact on the well-being of life on the earth and has reached a crisis point. This word *crisis* is often viewed in a negative way. However, it has two very different meanings—danger and opportunity. I believe that at this moment in history, it is important that we do not allow the more negative aspect of the word *crisis* to render us impotent, but that we instead engage with both its meanings, so that we may play a part in shaping the future. It may be overwhelming to realise that the choices each of us makes will influence the future unfolding of life on this planet. In spite of the deep crisis present at this time, I believe that humankind is, nevertheless, in a stronger position than ever to radically change its relationship with the planet.

How each of us responds is both our challenge and our gift to the future of life on the planet. Understanding ourselves as ancestors of the future generations offers us a larger context in which to locate our lives and to begin to see that the choices we make now matter greatly and will determine the gifts and legacies that these future beings will inherit from us. So how do you and I begin to make informed choices and so become empowered human beings who can act as agents of transformation?

Christopher Fry's poem "The Sleep of Prisoners" clearly outlines the crisis that we, as a society, face at this moment and also the challenge inherent in this time:

Thank God our time is now
When wrong comes up to meet us everywhere
Never to leave us until we take
The longest stride of soul men ever took.
Affairs are now soul size
The enterprise
Is exploration into God.
Where are you making for? It takes
So many thousand years to wake.
But will you wake for pity's sake?[1]

Fry suggests that one of the great challenges of our time is to
wake up—awaken to the truth of who we are and what it means
to be human.

In spite of the many ecological, human, and spiritual problems present in our world, there are indications that a radical transformation is possible in the way we humans perceive
ourselves and live on the planet. There is a belief that where
three streams of water come together, a place of special power
emerges. Likewise, where three streams of thinking converge,
a confluence of potent energy also exists. The following three
streams of thought are converging at this time and may have
the capacity to evoke a radical shift in the relationship between
humans and the rest of life on this planet:

The growing awareness of the present ecological crisis, cou-
pled with an increasing anguish over the future of the planet

The New Cosmology, with its understanding of the radical
interdependence of all life and the knowledge that we are part
of an emerging, dynamic, and creative universe that is neither
random nor predetermined

A re-emergence of the wisdom held in many ancient spiritual paths

The convergence of these three streams can awaken us to a more compelling story on which to base our lives. It can enable us to relocate our place and role within this evolving universe. People from different cultures will connect, in a special way, with the perennial truths present within their own traditions. This has already begun, and many people are reconnecting with the primal spiritual practices and stories of their ancestors. Thus, for people whose ancestry is within the Celtic and pre-Celtic traditions, they will reconnect with the perennial wisdom of that tradition as it evolved through its many phases throughout the millennia.

Cultural historian Thomas Berry suggests that the most significant task for the human population at this time is the creation of a sustainable future on this planet. He believes that our future depends on our ability to develop healthy relationships between human beings and the earth.[2] This requires a radical change in our understanding of the earth, our origins within it, and our deep interconnections within the fabric of the earth.

The Celtic spiritual tradition that has been handed down since the time of the Druids is deeply ecological. It understands that the earth is a sacred living being and emphasises the importance of human beings living in right relationship with the earth. John Scotus Erigena, a ninth century Irish philosopher, used the term *natura* to describe humans in relationship with their environment.[3] Humans exist only in the natural world, he believed, and therefore, to define human life without regard to our natural surroundings is impossible. I believe that re-embracing this ancient wisdom has the capacity to support us and guide us back into alignment with ourselves and with our mother, the earth. However, it will not be sufficient for us to reclaim this tradition as it was expressed in a former time. We must not only engage with this wisdom, but also encourage a dialogue with the current cosmology and scientific knowledge, so that a new flowering of the Celtic spiritual tradition can happen, one that will lead to an appropriate expression of its perennial wisdom in the present time.

Quantum physics assures us that, at a subatomic level, no separation exists within the created world. It speaks, in scientific language, of a view of reality held by the mystics of all spiritual traditions—that within the universe, an unbroken wholeness exists. The new cosmic story tells of the radical interconnection of all living sentient beings within the planet and of the evolution of this universe in an unbroken chain of events since its beginning 15 billion years ago. In this new story, we learn that the future is not predetermined, but that its evolution is influenced by the myriad of choices made within the universe in each moment. The fact that we, humans, have a role in creating the future of this part of the universe might seem an overwhelming reality to us. Yet it is true.

The final stream flowing into the current confluence is the growing awareness of the daily ecological crisis happening on the planet. Something deep within our psyche knows that the present level of species extinction is unnatural, that the pollution of the seas with radioactivity is serious, and that the erosion of soil from overproduction and deforestation is unsustainable. The dominant voices in western society still assure us that things are fine. Many of us know they are not fine, yet wonder what we can do to stop the destruction of the planet. Perhaps now after the disillusionment caused by the financial meltdown, more people will trust their own inner knowing and will question the assumptions of the many vested interests that dominate our society.

Sadly, many people still believe that if they allowed themselves to feel the pain of destruction of the many life forms on the planet, it would overwhelm them. Yet it is our ability to feel the pain that is crucial to our becoming agents of transformation. Feeling the pain and acknowledging the grief can help us move past the apathy that keeps so many of us paralysed. It can free our energy sufficiently to ask deeper questions and find deeper solutions to the present problems. In order to do this effectively, we must be willing to stand still and, on occasion, to stop business as usual—standing still not only so that we can feel the pain, but also to allow the universe, with all its wonder, to break in on us, to shatter our limiting beliefs, and to create a greater context in which to live our lives. An ancient Celtic triad speaks of what is needed for true understanding: "An eye to see what is, a heart to feel what is, and the boldness that dares to follow what is." More than ever, we now need to move toward a deeper understanding of life and, from that understanding, develop the boldness that dares to follow the heart. Each of us is called to play our unique part in this unfolding of life, each called to choose Life, as James Joyce invites us:

Welcome Oh Life
I go for the millionth time into the reality of experience
To forge in the smitty of my soul
The uncreated conscience of my race.[4]

Going Further:
Spiritual Ceremonies and Rituals

The decline in organised religion has happened more recently in Ireland than in other countries. Although the causes of this decline are complex, the effects are clear: People have become disillusioned with the churches, and society has adopted increasingly secular attitudes, rooted in rampant materialism. In the past, organised religion tended to encourage its followers to remain in a parent-child relationship, thus limiting the depth of spiritual development possible within that system. Paradoxically, the growth of a more secular, materialistic society has brought a sense of liberation from organised religion that has opened the possibility for deeper spiritual journeys, but outside church structures.

For years, I have pondered why many church services lack true spiritual power. What is missing, I believe, is the ability to cross that bridge from the left-brain, analytical, time-constrained realm into the other dimensions of reality, where myth and ritual rule and spiritual transformation is possible. In search of that different way of knowing, many people are now gathering outside the churches to create rituals and ceremonies that mark special occasions in their life journeys and to mark time in new and ancient ways. Creating and participating in spiritual practices, rituals, and ceremonies—alone or with other people—is central to the soul's journey. It can revitalise the spiritual dimensions of life and lead to the deepening of the spiritual life of individuals and the community.

Ritual in everyday life
The word *ritual* can often evoke fear or a sense of strangeness, conjuring all types of weird images and ideas. Yet our lives are filled with rituals. Some are secular in nature; others are spiritual; some are personal; others, communal. A ritual can be

created to mark any occasion, allowing us to be conscious of a particular event or time. We can introduce ritual into our daily lives by choosing to perform one or two activities in a conscious way, thereby creating simple, personal rituals.

However, to understand the role that personal and communal rituals play in our spiritual lives, we need to look more closely at what exactly I mean by ritual. Spiritual ritual is associated with the mythological dimension of life. Myth creates ritual, and ritual creates myth. Most rituals emerge from an underlying myth, which later becomes grounded in the ritual. The myth holds the essential truths underpinning the society or group and the norms of behaviour within that group, across the generations. A ritual thus is a myth turned into action.

Ritual works on two levels, the psychological and the spiritual. Rituals create a safe container in which we can experience the wonder, mystery, joy, and pain of our human existence along with that of the planet where we live and the universe that is our home. A ritual can reach the deeper layers of psyche, where true knowing resides, a region that is not accessible to the light of reason or the power of will. This is the soul level, that essential part of each of us, and it is to this aspect of the human that ritual relates.

Thomas Moore says that the soul prefers the imagination and that when the imagination is allowed to move to deep places, the sacred is revealed.[1] In this sense, ritual acts as a bridge between the ordinary plane of existence and the other dimensions of reality, for true ritual involves a journey into the otherworld dimension, where healing and transformation are possible. It is a journey into the heart, leading us to the inner realms of the psyche and ultimately to the soul or ground of being. We step away from the ordinary, mundane world and let go of rational and logical thinking so that we can enter into the mystery present within the ritual and experience the realm of the imaginal and the sacred. With Patrick Kavanagh, we recognise that head knowledge alone will never lead to the truth: "And I have a feeling that through a hole in reason's ceiling we can fly to knowledge without ever going to college."[2] When we re-emerge into ordinary reality, some element of ourselves will have been transformed.

Creating rituals—A beginner's guide

Creating new rituals for major life events and transitions is a very important task in our time. To do this effectively, though, it is necessary to understand some basic principles: While new rituals can evolve, and old rituals can be rediscovered and adapted for a particular purpose, authentic ritual must well up from within the psyche and cannot be constructed exclusively from a blueprint or template. A new ritual should relate to the life event being marked and draw from a valid tradition, yet also allow space for fresh ideas. For example, to celebrate the festival of Samhain within the Celtic tradition, first familiarise yourself with the festival's mythology and ritual practices. Next, having identified one or more key themes, devise appropriate ways to enact those themes. Genuine ritual, like symbols, cannot be invented by the logical mind. It must well up within us—often in dreams, daydreams, or meditations. Insights about the ritual may come to you out of the blue. However, you should resist the temptation to mix together lots of ideas that may sound great, but that are not directly connected with the ritual theme.

The creation of and participation in all true ritual requires discipline, patience, and perseverance—plus the ability to take ourselves lightly. Remember that you are engaging with a deep process and enlisting the support of the unseen worlds, with their various guides and energies, in order to bring the intentions held in the ritual into material form. Therefore, be respectful of the energies you are invoking and do not treat rituals in a trivial way. That does not mean that you have to be very serious and po-faced, just respectful.

Rituals can be private or public. Most of this guide refers to public ritual, but you can adapt the principles to your own personal ritual efforts. Public ritual needs an overall structure with guidelines to hold the ritual and bind participants together, but it must not be limited by these rules. The ritual must be allowed to transcend its frame. A dance needs to develop between the given and the possible, for this is how rituals not only transmit ancient knowledge, but also assist in the discovery of new knowledge. The flow of new understanding into the ritual ensures its vitality; it becomes a living link between the mundane and the spiritual, rather than a dry structure.

There are three stages to any ritual: the preparation, the actions of the actual ritual, and the conclusion and subsequent reflection. You should also build into your planning an opportunity to review what happened at the ritual and incorporate those insights into your next event.

Preparing for the ritual

The key to the preparation phase of ritual is to reach clarity as to the purpose and function of the ritual, since they will influence its structure. Once the purpose is clear, the essential quality held within the ritual will crystallise, and the appropriate words and actions will emerge. The prayers, songs, dances, chants, and actions to be used in the ritual are selected at this stage. It is best to use your own words, as this makes the ritual more personal and real. If you become unclear about the function of the ritual or if too many diverse aspects are creeping in, then stop, go back, check out the purpose of the ritual, and regain that initial clarity. You can then eliminate those aspects of the ritual that seem incongruent or nonessential.

Preparation can also involve reaching out to those who will join in the ritual. It is a universal law that energy follows intention; therefore, keep the intention of the ritual and your thoughts about it clear, especially as you communicate plans for the ritual. It is through shared intention that a ritual holds power and becomes real and alive for the people present. One way to involve participants in the preparation phase is by asking them to bring something personal to place on the altar or centrepiece planned for the ritual space, which should reflect the theme of the ritual.

Conducting a ritual

The first action on the day of the ritual is to create the space in which the ritual work will take place. This is usually a circle, but sometime it can be a square. Mark out an area with flowers, herbs, flour, cornmeal, stones, sticks, or other objects that are meaningful in the context of the ritual. The space can be "cleared" by using water and sage, together with prayers, to remove any negative energies that may hamper the ritual. Alternatively, you can create a ritual space simply by inviting people to stand or sit around the circle or square.

As people enter the space, sage or incense can be used to remove any heavy stresses so that participants enter with clear energy. You may want to use drumming or quiet reflective music to help people leave the outside world behind and cross the bridge into the mythical dimension. Once all have assembled, the sacred circle or square can be activated by calling in the major directions—East, South, West, and North; the sky above; the earth beneath; and the mystical centre—with prayers invoking the qualities and energies associated with each direction.

Next, a simple centring exercise can allow people to experience their connection with the earth and the heavens through their bodies and become more aware of the energy connecting these two realms. Many of the meditations in this book begin with such an exercise.

Finally, it is time for the prayers, songs, dances, and ritual actions that have been prepared! These take place in a predetermined sequence that takes participants into the mythical realm and then brings them back, transformed. This is where the balance between the prearranged form and the spontaneity that arises within the ritual must be held, so that the most authentic ritual emerges. This becomes easier with practice.

Concluding the ritual

The final procedure is to thank and release all the energies and directions that were present, along with the sacred space itself. The energies that created the space and that worked with us in the ritual should be present only for the duration of the ritual. This is especially true if the place where you are holding the ritual is used for other purposes. You can use simple, even spontaneous words of gratitude and dismissal.

All of the props you have used should also be thanked and returned to the appropriate places— flowers to the garden, for example. Holy well water can be given to people to take home or used to water the plants. All objects from the altar should be returned to their owners with respect and gratitude. Sharing the cleanup can itself be part of the ritual, followed by food and drinks. This celebration always enhances any ritual!

If you form a ritual group, it is helpful to include feedback sessions to check which aspects worked well and which did not. It is best not to do this feedback immediately after the ritual, because that will bring the event into the realm of the logical too quickly and dilute the enjoyable effects of the ritual. It might be appropriate to hold the feedback session at the beginning of the planning for the next ritual. Having a notebook where you record insights and reflections from your rituals is very useful, whether you are working in a ritual group or alone.

More ideas for rituals

Celebrating the festivals of the Celtic year is a wonderful way to build your ritual repertoire. Here are some ideas to inspire your ritual preparations and personal practice:

Study and learn about the many facets of time and how it manifests in our lives and in the worlds.

Become familiar with the concepts of time held by people from other eras and civilizations.

Find your own simple ways to honour the energy and associated tasks present in each season. Notice which energies are easy and which are difficult for you to embrace.

Create a simple altar in your home to reflect and honour the energy present in each season.

Create moments in each day, week, and year when you step outside of linear time to allow yourself to move into the infinite and eternal dimensions of reality.

Create your own unique prayers to support you and the tasks to be undertaken in each season.

Find a story or myth associated with the particular season, read it slowly, mull it over, and respond to the story in your own creative way using crayons, paints, clay, wool, words, poems, sounds, or whatever feels appropriate.

Visit and spend quiet time, alone and with others, at sacred places in the landscape, especially those associated with specific festivals. If you live in Ireland, for example, you might visit the Hill of Tara at Samhain, Newgrange at the time of the winter solstice, Sliabh Na Cailleach at the spring and autumn equinoxes, and Lough Gur at the summer solstice.

Find a place in your own locality to watch the sun rise on the Celtic festival days. Seek out and visit other nearby places where you feel particular resonances with different festivals and seasons.

Why do rituals work?

Creating appropriate rituals within our lives is powerful spiritual work that is urgently needed at this time. We may wonder, though: Why do rituals work? It is, I believe, because rituals and symbols speak the language of the unconscious and communicate with us at a much deeper level than we could achieve or even imagine with our conscious minds. Through ritual, we create a special safe and sacred space. Into this space, we can invoke help and support from our spirit guides, guardian angels, ancestors, the Christ, Our Lady, Brigid, or the Buddha energy. In this way it is possible for us to tap into the vast energies present in the universe and use them in a transformative way within. Each of us can engage with this work either on our own or as part of a group.

NOTES

Chapter 1 — Introduction
1 My story—everybody's story.
2 Thomas Berry, *The Dream of the Earth* (San Francisco: Sierra Publications, 1988), 4.

Chapter 2 — Who Are the Celtic People?
1 Seán Ó Duinn, *Where Three Streams Meet: Celtic Spirituality* (Dublin: Columba Press, 2000), 12.
2 Michael Dames, *Mythic Ireland* (London: Thames and Hudson, 1992), 9.
3 T. W. Rolleston, *Myths & Legends of the Celtic Race* (London: Constable, 1911), 81.
4 Rolleston, 82.
5 Shirley Toulson, *The Celtic Alternative: The Christianity We Lost* (London: Century Books, 1987), 9.
6 Seán Ó Duinn lecture notes (Dublin: 1993).
7 Rolleston, 90.
8 Ó Duinn, 18.
9 Rolleston, 35.
10 Rolleston, 91.
11 Rolleston, 93.
12 The Elders, Oraibi Arizona Hopi Nation communication (2002).

Chapter 3 — A Different Way of Knowing
1 Alfred Adler as cited in Nigel Pennick, *Celtic Sacred Landscapes* (London: Thames & Hudson, 1996), 7.
2 Seán Ó Duinn, lecture notes (1993).
3 Patrick Kavanagh, *The Complete Poems* (Newbridge, Ireland: Goldsmith Press, 1984), 256.
4 Joseph Campbell as cited in Matthew Fox, *Creation Spirituality: Liberating Gifts for the Peoples of the Earth* (San Francisco: Harper SanFrancisco, 1991), 30-31.
5 Information on the Céile Dé order is available at http://www.ceilede.co.uk.
6 David Spangler, "Between Order and Chaos: The Dynamic Realm Between Individualism and Mystical Unity," *In Context* 34 (Winter 1993), 55.
7 John Matthews, *The Celtic Shaman: A Handbook* (Shaftesbury, Dorset: Element, 1991), 32.
8 Carl G. Jung as cited in Rollo May, *The Cry for Myth* (London: Souvenir Press, 1991), 63.
9 Michael Dames, *Mythic Ireland* (London: Thames and Hudson, 1992), 257.

10 John Keats, letter to Benjamin Bailey, November 22, 1817, in *The Complete Poetical Works and Letters of John Keats* (Boston: Houghton, Mifflin & Co., 1899), 274.

11 Alwyn Rees & Brinley Rees, *Celtic Heritage: Ancient Tradition in Ireland and Wales* (London: Thames and Hudson, 1961), 341.

12 Rees & Rees, 344.

13 Kavanagh, 295.

Chapter 4 — Recovering the God-Intoxicated Celt

1 Teilhard de Chardin as cited in Bob Kelly. *Worth Repeating: More Than 5000 Classic and Contemporary Quotes* (Grand Rapids, MI: Kregel, 2003), 321.

2 Seán Ó Duinn, *Where Three Streams Meet: Celtic Spirituality* (Blackrock, Ireland: Columba Press, 2000), 164.

3 Ó Duinn, 166.

4 Ó Duinn, 167.

5 Ó Duinn, 169.

6 John Macquarrie, *Paths in Spirituality* (New York: Harper & Row, 1972), 122-3.

7 David Wagoner, *Traveling Light: Collected and New Poems* (Urbana, IL: University of Illinois Press, 1999), 10.

8 William Blake, *The Marriage of Heaven and Hell* (New York: Dover, 1994), 14.

9 Nigel Pennick, *Celtic Sacred Landscapes* (London: Thames & Hudson, 1996), 8.

10 Whitley Stokes, *The Martyrology of Oengus the Culdee* (London: Harrison & Sons, 1905), 65.

11 Noel Dermot O'Donoghue, *The Mountain Behind the Mountain: Aspects of the Celtic Tradition* (Edinburgh: T&T Clark, 1993), 81.

Chapter 5 — Celtic Christian Spirituality: A Holy Embrace of Spirit and Nature

1 Alwyn Rees & Brinley Rees, *Celtic Heritage: Ancient Tradition in Ireland and Wales* (London: Thames & Hudson, 1961), 98.

2 Translated probably by Seán Ó Tuathail for *Cainteanna na Luise: Journal of Modern Druidic Arts* (Toronto: 1984/1986).

3 H. J. Massingham as cited in Christopher Bamford & William Parker Marsh, *Celtic Christianity: Ecology and Holiness* (Edinburgh: Floris Books, 1986), 19.

4 Seán Ó Duinn, *Insight into Gaelic Spirituality* [lecture notes] (Dublin: All Hallow's College, 1991).

5 John J. Ó Ríordáin, *The Music of What Happens* (Dublin: Columba Press, 1996), 45-46.

6 Seán Ó Duinn, *Where Three Streams Meet: Celtic Spirituality* (Dublin: Columba Press, 2005), 179.

7 Kathleen Raine as cited in Noel Dermot O'Donoghue, *The Mountain Behind the Mountain: Aspects of the Celtic Tradition* (Edinburgh: T&T Clark, 1993), 29.

8 Patrick Kavanagh, *The Complete Poems* (Newbridge, Ireland: Goldsmith Press, 1984), 205.

9 Thomas Berry, *The Dream of the Earth* (San Francisco: Sierra Publications, 1988), xiv.
10 Rees & Rees, 74.
11 Ó Duinn, *Where Three Streams Meet*, 87.
12 Shirley Toulson, *The Celtic Alternative: The Christianity We Lost* (London: Century Books, 1987), 65.
13 Toulson, 65.
14 Toulson, 61.
15 Robin Flower, *The Irish Tradition* (Dublin: Lilliput Press, 1994), 42.
16 Seán Ó Duinn, Lecture notes at All Hallows College (Dublin: 1991).
17 Deuteronomy 11:13-15.
18 Toulson, 66.
19 Toulson, 64.
20 Toulson, 9.
21 H. J. Massingham as cited in Bamford & Marsh, 10.
22 Ó Duinn, *Where Three Streams Meet*, 35.
23 Alexander Carmichael, *Carmina Gadelica: Hymns and Incantations* (Edinburgh: Floris Books, 1992), 96-97.
24 Carmichael, *Carmina Gadelica*, 344-346.
25 Carmichael, *Carmina Gadelica*, 287.
26 Carmichael, *Carmina Gadelica*, 291-292.
27 Alexander Carmichael, *The Sun Dances* (Edinburgh: Floris Books, 1988), 57.
28 Caitlin Matthews, *The Little Book of Celtic Blessings* (Shaftesbury, U.K.: Element, 1994), 11.
29 Matthews, 30.
30 Matthews, 22.
31 Matthews, 23.
32 Bamford & Marsh, 47.

Chapter 6 — The Divine Feminine in Celtic Spirituality

1 Proinsias Mac Cana, *Celtic Mythology* (Feltham, U.K.: Newnes, 1983), 34-35.
2 Pádraigín Clancy, "St. Brigid of Ireland: From Pagan Goddess to Christian Saint," *Africa Magazine* (St. Patrick's Missionary Society, Kiltegan, Ireland: 1994).
3 Alexei Kondratiev, *Celtic Rituals: A Guide to Ancient Celtic Spirituality* (Doughcloyne, Ireland: Collins Press, 2004), 137.
4 Seán Ó Duinn, *The Rites of Brigid: Goddess and Saint* (Dublin: Columba Press, 2005), 67.
5 Rita Minehan, *Rekindling the Flame* (Kildare, Ireland: Solas Bhride Community, 1999).
6 Brat Bhride is a Dundalk based group who organise an annnul Brigid Festival details on www.bratbhride.com
7 Mary T. Condren, "*Brigit: Soulsmith for the New Millennium*" (2000), http://instituteforfeminismandreligion.org.
8 Cogitosus, *Life of Saint Brigit*.
9 Seán Ó Duinn, *Where Three Streams Meet: Celtic Spirituality* (Blackrock, Ireland: Columba Press, 2000), 88.

10 Esther Hicks &, Jerry Hicks, *The Amazing Power of Deliberate Intent: Living the Art of Allowing* (London: Hay House, 2008).

11 Alwyn Rees & Brinley Rees, *Celtic Heritage: Ancient Tradition in Ireland and Wales* (London: Thames & Hudson, 1961), 73.

12 Kondratiev, 106.

13 Helena Roerich as cited in Jacqueline Decter, *Nicholas Roerich* (Rochester, VT: Park Street Press), 190.

14 La Lugh, *"Brighid's Kiss"* (CD, 1995).

Chapter 7 — The Celtic Year Calendar

1 Alwyn Rees & Brinley Rees, *Celtic Heritage: Ancient Tradition in Ireland and Wales* (London: Thames & Hudson, 1961), 88.

2 Rees & Rees, 88.

3 Noel Dermot O'Donoghue, *The Mountain Behind the Mountain: Aspects of the Celtic Tradition* (Edinburgh: T&T Clarke, 1993), 16-17.

4 Seán Ó Duinn, *Where Three Streams Meet: Celtic Spirituality* (Dublin: Columba Press, 2000), 246.

5 Ó Duinn, 241.

Chapter 8 — Celebrating the Celtic Seasons

1 Michael Dames, *Mythic Ireland* (London: Thames and Hudson, 1992), 247.

2 Alexei Kondratiev, *Celtic Rituals: A Guide to Ancient Celtic Spirituality* (Doughcloyne, Ireland: Collins Press, 2004), 106.

3 Kondratiev, 107.

4 Fionn Tulach, *"Notes on An Latha Bhride (Bridget's Day) 1st-2nd Feb"* (2005), http://www.ceilede.co.uk/articles/Bhride.pdf.

5 Kondratiev, 137.

6 Kondratiev, 139.

7 Kondratiev, 139.

8 Kondratiev, 161.

9 Kondratiev, 174.

10 Kondratiev, 170.

Chapter 9 — The Rhythm of Life Is a Powerful Beat

1 D. H. Lawrence, "A Propos of *Lady Chatterley's Lover"* in *Lady Chatterley's Lover* (New York: Bantam, 1968), 361.

2 Alexei Kondratiev, *Celtic Rituals: A Guide to Ancient Celtic Spirituality* (Doughcloyne, Ireland: Collins Press, 2004), 97.

3 John J. Ó Ríordáin, *The Music of What Happens* (Blackrock, Ireland: Columba Press, 1996), 7.

4 Philip Carr-Gomm, *The Elements of the Druid Tradition* (Shaftesbury, U.K.: Element, 1991), 74.

5 Kahlil Gibran, *The Prophet* (London: Heinemann, 1926), 12.

6 David Whyte, *Where Many Rivers Meet: Poems* (Langley, Washington: Many

Rivers Press, 1990), 35.

7 M. Louise Haskins, *The Gate of the Year* (London: Hodder and Stoughton, 1940).

Epilogue
1 Christopher Fry as cited in Jean Houston, *The Possible Human: A Course in Extending Your Physical, Mental, and Creative Abilities* (Los Angeles: J.P. Tarcher, 1982), xi.
2 Thomas Berry, *The Dream of the Earth* (San Francisco: Sierra Publications, 1988).
3 John Scotus Erigena, *Periphyseon*.
4 James Joyce as cited in Rollo May, *The Courage to Create* (New York: Bantam Books, 1976), 20.

Going Further: Spiritual Ceremonies and Rituals
1 Thomas Moore, *Care of the Soul: How to Add Depth and Meaning to Your Everyday Life* (New York: Harper Collins, 1992), xx.
2 Patrick Kavanagh, *The Complete Poems* (Newbridge, Ireland: Goldsmith Press, 1984), 288.

Bibliography

Agnew, Una,
    The Mystical Imagination of Patrick Kavanagh
    (Dublin: Columba Press, 1998).

Bamford, Christopher, & William Parker Marsh,
    Celtic Christianity: Ecology and Holiness
    (Edinburgh: Floris Books, 1986).

Berry, Thomas,
    The Dream of the Earth
    (San Francisco: Sierra Publications, 1988).
_____, *The Great Work* (New York: Bell Tower, 1999).

Blamires, Steve,
    Celtic Tree Mysteries
    (St. Paul, MN: Llewellyn Publications, 2003).
_____, *The Irish Magical Tradition* (London: Aquarian Press, 1992).

Broomfield, John,
    Other Ways of Knowing
    (Rochester, VT: Inner Traditions, 1997).

Campbell, Joseph,
    The Hero With a Thousand Faces
    (London: Paladin Books, 1949).
_____, *Myths to Live By* (London: Souvenir Press, 1973).

Carmichael, Alexander,
    Carmina Gadelica: Hymns and Incantations
    (Edinburgh: Floris Books, 1992).
_____, *New Moon of the Seasons* (Edinburgh: Floris Books, 1986).
_____, *The Sun Dances* (Edinburgh: Floris Books, 1988).

Carr-Gomm, Philip,
    The Elements of the Druid Tradition
    (Shaftesbury, Dorset: Element Books, 1991).

Carr-Gomm, Philip (Ed.),
    The Druid Renaissance
    (London: Thorsons, 1996).
    Celtic Mythology
    (New Lanark, Scotland: Geddes & Grosset, 1999).

Clancy, Padraigin (Ed.),
    Celtic Threads
    (Dublin: Veritas Publications, 1999).

Condren, Mary,
    The Serpent and the Goddess
    (San Francisco: Harper & Row, 1989).

Cousineau, Phil,
    The Art of Pilgrimage
    (Berkeley, CA: Conari Press, 1998).

Dames, Michael,
    Mythic Ireland
    (London: Thames & Hudson, 1992).

Fox, Matthew,
    The Coming of the Cosmic Christ
    (San Francisco: Harper & Row, 1988).
_____, *Creation Spirituality: Liberating Gifts for the Peoples of
    the Earth* (San Francisco: HarperSanFrancisco, 1991).
_____, *Original Blessing* (Santa Fe, NM: Bear & Co., 1983).
_____, *Spirituality Called Compassion*
    (Minneapolis, MN: Winston Press, 1979).

Fox, Matthew (Ed.),
   Western Spirituality
   (Santa Fe, NM: Bear & Co., 1981).

Flower, Robin,
   The Irish Tradition
   (Dublin: Lilliput Press, 1994).

Harding, Esther,
   Woman's Mysteries
   (London: Rider, 1971).

Howell, Alice,
   The Dove in the Stone
   (Wheaton, IL: Quest Books, 1988).
_____, *The Web in the Sea* (Wheaton, IL: Quest Books, 1993).

Johnson, Robert,
   She
   (New York: Harper, 1989).

Kavanagh, Patrick,
   Collected Poems
   (London: Penguin, 2004).
_____, *Complete Poems* (Newbridge, Ireland: Goldsmith Press, 1984).

Kondratiev, Alexei,
   Celtic Rituals: A Guide to Ancient Celtic Spirituality
   (Doughcloyne, Ireland: Collins Press, 2004).

Mac Cana, Proinsias,
   Celtic Mythology
   (London: Hamlyn, 1970).

McColman, Carl,
   366 Celt
   (London: Element, 2005).

McIntosh, Alastair,
   Soil and Soul
   (London: Aurum Press, 2002).

Macleod, Fiona,
   Iona
   (Edinburgh: Floris, 1982).

Mahon, Bríd,
   Land of Milk and Honey
   (Dublin: Mercier Press, 1991).
_____, *While Green Grass Grows* (Dublin: Mercier Press, 1998).

Matthews, Caitlin,
   Elements of the Celtic Tradition
   (Shaftesbury, Dorset: Element, 1989).
_____, *The Little Book of Celtic Blessings*
   (Shaftesbury, Dorset: Element, 1994).

Matthews, Caitlin, & John Matthews,
   The Little Book of Celtic Wisdom
   (Shaftesbury, Dorset: Element, 1993).
_____, *The Western Way* (London: Arkana, 1994).

Matthews, John,
   The Celtic Shaman: A Handbook
   (Shaftesbury, Dorset: Element, 1991).

May, Rollo,
   The Courage to Create
   (New York: Bantam Books, 1976).
_____, *The Cry for Myth*
   (London: Souvenir Press, 1991).

Merry, Eleanor,
 The Flaming Door
 (Edinburgh: Floris Books, 1990).

Meehan, Cary,
 The Traveller's Guide to Sacred Ireland
 (Glastonbury: Gothic Image, 2002).

Moore, Thomas,
 Care of the Soul
 (New York: Harper Collins, 1992).

O'Connor, Peter,
 Beyond the Mist
 (London: Orion, 2001).

O'Donoghue, Noel Dermot,
  The Angels Keep Their Ancient Places
  (Edinburgh: T & T Clarke, 2001).
_____, *Heaven in Ordinarie*
  (Edinburgh: T & T Clarke, 1979).
_____, *The Mountain Behind the Mountain:*
  Aspects of the Celtic Tradition
  (Edinburgh: T&T Clark, 1993).

O'Donohue, John,
 Anam Cara
 (London: Bantam, 1997).
_____, *Benedictus* (London: Transworld, 2007).

Ó Duinn, Seán,
 The Rites of Brigid, Goddess and Saint
 (Dublin: Columba Press, 2005).
_____, *Where Three Streams Meet* (Dublin: Columba Press, 2000).

Ó hOgáin, Dáithí,
>   *Myth, Legend and Romance:*
>   *An Encyclopaedia of Irish Folk Tradition*
>   (New York: Prentice Hall, 1991).

Ó Ríordáin, John J.,
>   *The Music of What Happens*
>   (Dublin: Columba Press, 1996).

Pennick, Nigel,
>   *Celtic Sacred Landscapes*
>   (London: Thames & Hudson, 1996).

Rees, Alwyn, and Brinley Rees,
>   *Celtic Heritage: Ancient Tradition in Ireland and Wales*
>   (London: Thames & Hudson, 1961).

Roose-Evans, James,
>   *Passages of the Soul*
>   (Shaftesbury, Dorset: Element, 1995).

Rolleston, T. W.,
>   *Myths and Legends of the Celtic Race*
>   (London: Constable, 1911).

Rutherford, Ward,
>   *The Druids*
>   (Wellingborough, Northampshire: Aquarian Press, 1978).

Simpson, Ray,
>   *Soul Friendship*
>   (London: Hodder & Stoughton, 1999).

Smyth, Daragh,
>   *A Guide to Irish Mythology*
>   (Dublin: Irish Academic Press, 1988).

St Aubyn, Lorna,
Everyday Rituals and Ceremonies:
Special Ways to Mark Important Events in Your Life
(London: Piatkus, 1994).

Steiner, Rudolf,
The Druids
(Forest Row, East Sussex: Sophia Books, 2001).

Streit, Jakob,
Sun and Cross
(Edinburgh: Floris Books, 1984).

Stewart, R. J.,
Celtic Myths and Legends
(London: Blandford, 1996).

Toulson, Shirley,
The Celtic Alternative: The Christianity We Lost
(London: Century Books, 1987).
_____, *The Celtic Year*
(Shaftesbury, Dorset: Element, 1993).

Young, Ella,
Celtic Wonder Tales
(Edinburgh: Floris Books, 1985).

Ywahoo, Dhyani,
Voices of the Ancestors
(London: Shambhala Press, 1987).

Zaczek, Iain,
Chronicles of the Celts
(London: Collins & Brown, 1996).